THE LONG ROAD HOME

Adrian Vincent

This is a war book, but there are no heroes in it. Indeed, it might well be thought that much of what happens in it does not reflect greatly to anyone's credit. It is a study of men at each other's throats in a desperate battle for survival during long marches into and out of captivity as prisoners in enemy hands, and it is told with complete candour, and with no attempt to gloss over the facts. For this reason it is an important book, and was widely recognised as such on its first publication more than ten years ago. It makes compulsive reading.

Adrian Vincent

THE
LONG ROAD
HOME

HOWARD BAKER, LONDON

Adrian Vincent
THE LONG ROAD HOME

Originally published in Great Britain by
George Allen and Unwin Limited, 1956

This Howard Baker edition, 1970

A Howard Baker Book

SBN 09 304930 7

Howard Baker books are published by
Howard Baker Publishers Limited,
47 Museum Street, London, W.C.1.

Reproduced and Printed in Great Britain by
Redwood Press Limited, Trowbridge and London.
and bound in Wales by
Remploy Limited, Ystradgynlais, Glamorgan.

CONTENTS

CHAPTER ONE

The Fall of Calais

IN the early hours of a cold May morning in 1940, a battalion
of soldiers arrived at Dover. They were the first battalion of
the Queen Victoria's Rifles. Five days later nearly all of
them were either dead, wounded, or taken prisoner.

Like the rest of the men who stood on the quay that morning, I had no idea of what was in store for us. None of us
even knew that the boat waiting there was due to take us to
Calais, and even if we had known it, none of us would have
been unduly worried. There had been nothing in the papers
to alarm anyone, and the war still seemed very far away.

Standing there, waiting to go up the gangplank, I suddenly realized how quickly the last five months had gone
and how in such a little time so much had happened. I remembered it all: the calling-up papers in January; the
arrival with the rest of the conscripts at Paddock Wood,
trudging through the snow in our thin civilian shoes until
we had reached the cluster of oast-houses and hop-kilns
where the Queen Victoria's Rifles were stationed; the early
days of training in the frozen fields, dodging in and out
among the hop-frames, and the nights spent shivering in
the hop-kilns, with the snow falling gently through the ven-
tilator and melting on the solitary oil-stove that stood in the
centre of the kiln. I remembered the end of the training
period, the end of the winter, and the pleasant hours spent
on motor-bikes, tearing up and down the country lanes; the
evenings and week-ends spent in Tonbridge and Maid-
stone, promenading up and down the main streets making
passes at the giggling girls on the corners. I remembered the
departure from Paddock Wood, as the motor-bikes, the
side-cars, and the scout-cars went through the gates for the

last time, with the villagers waving farewell until we had all disappeared in a cloud of dust. I remembered the last stage of the journey before reaching this quay; the dog days of constant guard duty at Ashford, with nothing to do but stand for hours in front of the farms and empty houses where we were stationed, until that, too, had ended with a flurried departure at an hour's notice, with the bikes, the side-cars, and the scout-cars left standing at the roadside.

The suddenness of the departure, the abandoning of the vehicles, and with it the jettisoning of our training as a motor-cycle unit, should have warned us that something special was on. But as we had travelled through the night in the stuffy railway carriages, the conversations between the intermittent dozings had shown little sign of worry. It had not been much of a war so far. There had been a few raids, a few skirmishes, a few troops in action, but overseas there were still thousands doing nothing. There was no reason to think that we would not be joining them. Patrol work in some nice safe area was the final conclusion. Nothing really dangerous, nothing to be worried about.

Not long afterwards we were all aboard and the ship was slipping gently away from the side of the quay. We waved to the dockers until we were out of the harbour, and then we were watching the cliffs of Dover gradually recede into the mist. On the upper deck, a Bren gunner crouched behind his gun, scanning the sky.

Half-way across, Company meetings were held in the cabins. We were going to Calais. There was trouble on the other side; there had been a break-through, and we were to hold positions leading into the town and to guard the beaches. These few bald statements bore no relation to what we had been reading in the papers, and it was therefore not surprising that we had little difficulty in persuading ourselves that our officers were probably unduly dramatizing the situation. It was only when we reached Calais and heard the guns thudding in the distance that we realized that the situation really was serious.

While we stood around on the quay waiting for the ammunition and equipment to be unloaded, I tried to talk to some of the French dockers. They did not seem very friendly—in fact, they were almost hostile. I was therefore not very surprised when I heard later that they had gone on strike the next day in the middle of unloading the stores of the King's Royal Rifle Corps and the Rifle Brigade who had come to join us.

It was only towards the end of our brief campaign, after we had been harassed by French Fifth Columnists, had heard of French and Belgian soldiers held captive by our own troops, and had observed the complete moral disintegration of the French and Belgian troops who had fled into Calais, that we realized that phrases like 'the *Entente Cordiale*' and 'allied solidarity' no longer meant anything.

But at that moment there was only the distant thudding of guns to disturb us. Meanwhile, most of the equipment had been unloaded. There was not much of it; 40 Bren guns and 20 anti-tank guns for a whole battalion. Two-thirds of the ranks had rifles and none too much ammunition, while the rest had only pistols and a few rounds each.

Eventually, platoons began to move off in different directions, and some hours later I found myself with my own platoon, standing among some sand-dunes that overlooked one of the beaches. By then it was nearly dusk and the guns had stopped firing. To the left of us was the town of Calais, looking so quiet and peaceful with the sun setting behind it, that it was difficult to realize that for us the war was now something more than headlines in a newspaper. Taking up a position among the dunes, I watched the dusk gradually deepen into darkness, until all I could see was the shadowy outline of the man nearest me. Around us, the clumps of grass sprouting out of the sand rustled dryly in the night breeze. Below, the sea lapped gently on the beach. Nothing else disturbed the silence.

The next morning, the officer in charge of the platoon disappeared in the direction of the town. While we waited among the sand-dunes, smoking the last of our cigarettes, we heard the guns again. They sounded much nearer than they had done the day before. Although we did not know it, the Germans were already less than nine miles from Calais.

When the officer returned, he brought with him the information that we had been ordered to guard a road-block that had already been set up for us on one of the roads leading into Calais. As we marched away from the sand-dunes, we watched a solitary British plane slowly circle the town and then head out to sea. Despite the guns, everything still seemed peaceful enough.

Some hours later we were standing on a road outside Calais, looking at a couple of handcarts drawn across the road in front of us. They did not look as if they could stop a couple of determined German foot soldiers, let alone a tank. Seeing the expression on some of our faces, the officer explained that we were not holding the road-block as a defensive position, but merely as a check-point. At the first sign of the enemy, we would move. Everyone suddenly looked a little more cheerful. The officer then went on to explain our duties at the road-block. All civilian refugees were to be turned back and French and Belgian military personnel allowed to pass only if they could produce their identification papers. There were to be no exceptions.

Leaving two men on guard at the road-block, the officer led the way towards a small farm that stood at the edge of the road a few yards behind the barricade. As we marched into the yard, the owner of the farm shuffled forward to meet us. He was a very old man, probably getting on for eighty, with a lined and weather-beaten face almost hidden by an aggressive white moustache. It was evident that he was delighted to have us, and after much handshaking and a certain amount of embracing, suffered with embarrassed fortitude by most of the platoon, we followed him into the house.

Once we were inside the white-washed kitchen, the old

man produced a bottle of cognac and some glasses, and we all settled down at the table. We drank to the downfall of Germany; we drank to France; we drank to England; and then we drank to the downfall of Germany again. After that we kept drinking to the downfall of Germany until the bottle was empty. By that time the atmosphere in the room was distinctly merry.

All at once the old man got up and went out of the room, leaving us to forage around for any food that we could find. He returned a few minutes later with an imposing array of medals pinned on his chest, saluted us a little unsteadily, and then in a loud voice announced his intention of fighting by our side at the barricade. He seemed disappointed to hear we had no intention of making a last stand there. To console him, we admired his medals at great length, and then gravely examined his battle-scars received in the colonial wars.

Later that day the first refugees arrived, trudging slowly down the road towards us. There were about a dozen of them, mostly middle-aged or old people, who had come from the nearby farms, leaving everything behind them in their flight. Several very young children were with them, walking quietly along with that rather adult self-possession that most French children seem to have. Reaching the barricade, the refugees came to a halt and waited for us to move the carts out of the way. The three of us on duty at the barricade braced ourselves for the unpleasant task of turning them back.

'*Vous ne pouvez passer,*' I said quietly.

What followed was painful to say the least of it. While the three of us stood there, shaking our heads and muttering '*Vous ne pouvez passer*' in a rather shame-faced chorus, the men cursed us solidly, while their women stood beside them sobbing. To make matters worse, an old peasant woman dropped to her knees begging to be allowed to join her relatives in the town, until finally two men dragged her to her feet. For a long time after that they stood around the barricade in little groups, watching us in silence, obviously hoping that we would relent and let them pass through. At dusk they finally gave up and began to make their way back along the road. Soon the road was quite deserted again.

It was also on that afternoon that the 2nd Battalion of the King's Royal Rifle Corps arrived at Calais, together with the 1st Battalion of the Rifle Brigade. Like the troops already in the town, they had been given no real picture of what was going on in France or why they had been sent to Calais.

Whatever knowledge any of the officers might have had of the true purpose of the impending battle, they kept it to themselves. The original intention, it transpired, was to hold Calais and to keep it open as a port for the B.E.F., and also to establish a line of communication with Dunkirk. By the time we had arrived, however, the situation had deteriorated so much that this was no longer possible. Our task then became that of engaging the German 1st and 10th Armoured Divisions in an attempt to divert them from the B.E.F. falling back on Dunkirk. Although this task was accomplished, very few of the troops, if any, knew that the B.E.F. was being evacuated at that time.

It was this lack of knowledge of what was happening, the seeming futility of fighting a senseless and losing battle with no air support and no ammunition worth talking about, that led to a great deal of bitterness among the troops who survived to talk about it.

The next day more refugees arrived, a great torrent of them this time, and with them came a sprinkling of French troops—exhausted, a little panic-stricken, and half of them without arms. We struggled for a while with the great mass at the barricade, trying to sort out the troops from the civilians, and then we gave up and they all passed through.

Later that day something happened at the barricade to change the usual routine. For the last few hours there had been a constant trickle of French troops and civilians, and we had dealt with them as best we could. But now the road was quiet again. Suddenly a car appeared in sight and moved slowly towards the barricade. As it halted, I walked forward with the other rifleman on duty with me. In the car was a Belgian officer and a woman. The woman was a blonde, about thirty, and very attractive.

'*Papiers, s'il vous plaît,*' I said, sticking my hand through the window of the car.

'No papers,' the Belgian officer said in English. 'All lost. We had to leave in a hurry.' He smiled. 'Does it matter? We are all comrades.'

'Not without papers, we're not,' I said.

The woman leaned over the officer and spoke, also in English. 'The Germans are very near. Do you know that?'

'So they tell me,' I said, trying to ignore the sudden lurching of my stomach. 'But we're not talking about the Germans at the moment. We're talking about identification papers, which this officer doesn't seem to have. What about you?'

'I have no papers,' the woman said. 'When you are fleeing for your life, you do not think of such things.'

'I'm sorry,' I said. 'But if you can't produce any identification papers, I can't let you through.'

They looked at each other and then the Belgian officer shrugged.

'The Germans are coming along this road now,' the woman said very quietly, 'and all you can think about is papers. Doesn't it frighten you that they may arrive at any moment?'

'No,' I lied. 'It doesn't.' With a cigarette drooping from my mouth and my helmet pushed on the back of my head, I hoped that I looked a little more nonchalant than I felt.

'You would be frightened,' the woman said, 'if you had seen what I have seen farther back—your comrades lying dead in the road. If you and your friend are wise, you will run away while you have the time, instead of bothering about papers.'

13

'Are you suggesting that we should desert our post?' I said slowly.

'Yes,' the woman said. 'I am. If you stay here you will be dead within a few hours. Run now, while you have the chance! Both of you!'

I unslung my rifle and poked it through the window of the car. 'You'd better call the officer,' I said to the rifleman beside me. 'Tell him I think we've got a couple of Fifth Columnists.'

The woman started to say something and then stopped as the Belgian officer patted her hand. He did not take his eyes off the rifle.

Out of the corner of my eye I watched the rifleman enter the farmyard, and then I turned my attention to the two occupants of the car. To be truthful, I was feeling rather pleased with myself. Already I could hear the officer commending me for my alertness. Perhaps, I thought happily, I might even receive a medal.

Poking my rifle farther through the window I said smugly: 'You certainly picked the wrong soldier this time, didn't you?'

The woman was about to say something, when a series of shattering explosions rattled the windows of the car. Swinging round, I saw great clods of earth rising high into the air, only a few yards from the farm. Almost before they had fallen, the whole platoon was out of the farm and making for the road. A stream of tracer shells pouring out of a small wood some five hundred yards away, sent earth showering into the yard of the farm. By the time the tanks appeared, nosing their way through the trees, I was already streaking down the road after the platoon, with no further thought of my two 'spies' or possible medals. Only afterwards, when I was safely around the bend of the road with the others, did I think again of the two in the car, and remembered the sardonic smile hovering on the Belgian officer's face as I pulled my rifle back out of the window and started to run.

We kept moving at a steady jog-trot until we had reached

a quiet road just outside the town. Flopping down on each side of the gravel road, we waited for the tanks to come. While I waited, hoping and praying that no tank would appear, I tried to reconcile our rapid and slightly undignified retreat with the absurdity of us now sitting around waiting for trouble in a spot even less advantageous than the farm.

But soon other things occupied my mind. Calais was no longer the quiet town it had been when we had arrived. Idly I watched two Messerschmitts chasing a Hurricane that looped and dived and slipped in a frantic effort to escape before it finally disappeared from sight, trailing behind it a cloud of dense black smoke. Quite near I could hear the shrill whine of a three-inch mortar, and mingling with it the more throaty roar of artillery thundering away somewhere outside the town. A great cloud of smoke rose high into the sky from Boulogne and then drifted slowly towards Calais. It was almost impossible to believe that only three days ago we were outside Ashford, with nothing more to complain about than the appalling boredom of continual guard duty.

For ages it seemed we waited, while all the time the noise of battle around Calais grew louder and louder, until we seemed to be surrounded by it. But nothing came along the road, and in the end we clambered to our feet again and began to make our way cautiously towards the *Gare Maritime*.

From the moment we left that road until nightfall, we were never out of trouble. Before we finally reached the docks, we had been fired on by French Fifth Columnists sniping at us from a deserted building; sheltered under some abandoned French trucks while mortar bombs exploded around us steadily for over an hour, and had crossed a piece of waste ground under Fifth Column fire, leaving behind us our first casualties lying quietly among the scrub. We arrived in the region of the *Gare Maritime* just in time to provide an additional target for a squadron of Stukas that had come over to bomb the docks.

I was very cautiously bringing up the rear of the platoon, when I became aware that I was alone, watching the first bombs drop, while some way ahead of me the rest of the platoon dived for cover under the shelter of a sloping bank that dropped down to the *Bassin de Chasses,* a great basin of water between the station and the beaches. With no time to join them, I went for cover under the nearest thing available, a solitary truck standing close to a high wall. For the next few minutes the air was full of the sound of the terrifying whine of the diving Stukas, the thudding of the bombs dropping, and machine-gun fire spattering along the quay, mingling into a hideous cacophony of sound that made me scrabble at the shuddering ground in what was purely a reflex action to dig myself deeper into it.

When it was all over I lay there for some time, gradually becoming conscious that the gravel was biting into my face. Slowly I lifted myself to my elbows, scraped the gravel from my face, and fumbled with shaking fingers for a cigarette. Finding only an empty packet, I crawled out from beneath the truck and found a Company-Sergeant-Major waiting to greet me.

The C.S.M. looked at me coldly. 'What do you think you've been doing under that truck, soldier?'

Under the circumstances, it struck me as a silly question, but politely and respectfully I said: 'Sheltering, sir.'

'You bloody fool,' the C.S.M. said without emotion. 'That's an ammunition truck.' He walked away, leaving me thoughtfully regarding the shrapnel scattered around the truck.

After that there was a welcome lull. Now that we had reached the *Gare Maritime,* no one seemed to have the slightest idea what the next move was to be. In the end I got tired of propping up the wall and went for a short walk along the quay. Farther along was another lorry, and on the tailboard of it lay the curled-up body of a British officer, shot through one of the buttocks. He lay like a child in the womb, his knees close to his stomach, his head low on his chest. Sitting down against the wall only a few inches away from the tailboard of the truck and the khaki figure with the blood spreading on its trousers, I opened my last tin of corned beef. I was hardly conscious of the figure on the tailboard.

Suddenly there was the crackle of small-arms fire, and a few moments later the C.S.M. came hurrying along, keeping close to the wall. Beckoning to me, and also to the two riflemen lounging against the wall nearby, to follow him, he turned back again, running lightly on his toes, hardly making a sound. Equally as quietly but with less enthusiasm, the three of us followed him. Reaching a break in the wall, the C.S.M. came to an abrupt halt. Drawing his revolver, he peered around the wall.

The next moment his head shot back again. 'Fix bayonets!' he said quietly.

Oh, my God, I thought, fumbling with my bayonet. Not hand-to-hand fighting with some dirty great German, finishing off the whole thing for me by driving his bayonet into my stomach. Fear, awful, paralysing fear, gripped me as I fixed my bayonet.

'Steady, boys,' the C.S.M. whispered encouragingly. 'And don't be frightened to use those bayonets. You've been taught how to handle them.'

We had. It was, however, one thing to charge a suspended straw sack, grimacing and grunting, stabbing and slashing, with a Sergeant yelling exhortations to 'stick the bastard' and 'rip him up', and quite another thing to stand behind a wall with the knowledge that at any moment a German who has gone through a similar drill, and is probably more efficient at it than you, might suddenly appear with nothing on his mind but the one thought of plunging *his* bayonet into your shrinking flesh. With my breath catching in my throat and my rifle held ready for a blind lunge, I waited,

17

expecting to hear at any moment the sound of jackboots thudding towards us.

But nothing disturbed the silence, and after we had waited there for a few minutes, the C.S.M. sidled around the wall and disappeared into the yard on the other side of it. As we had not been given any instructions to follow, the three of us stayed right where we were, expecting to hear the sound of shots that would be signal for us to dutifully rush forward and make our début with the bayonet. On the other side of the wall I could hear someone moving quietly around the yard. I hoped it was the C.S.M.

The C.S.M. suddenly reappeared. 'All right, boys,' he said casually, replacing his revolver in its holster. 'You can put your bayonets away. It was a false alarm.'

Speechless, the three of us watched him stalk away. And then the anticlimax of it all was suddenly too much for us. We started to giggle, our laughter growing in volume, until in the end we were all leaning against the wall, roaring with laughter. It was quite some time before we were in a fit state to join the others.

Just before dusk we moved on towards the docks, walking slowly in a single file along the basin, trying not to look at the occasional dead body that lay huddled among the tangled grass that dropped down to the water. Behind us, blazing buildings lit the sky with a pink glow, across which trailed great wisps of smoke that drifted slowly over the burning town and then out to sea.

Reaching the dock area, we began to meet other troops moving out of the town. Hoping that perhaps they could tell us something that would make sense out of the whole business, we mingled with them, asking them what they knew about the situation. They knew nothing; only that they had no water, no food, little ammunition, and that the Fifth Column was everywhere, sniping from houses, shops, and churches. They were very bitter about the Fifth Column, and told us stories of French and Belgian soldiers being held prisoners by British troops, who had orders to shoot if they tried to escape. It seemed that although most of the Fifth Columnists were Germans who had filtered through into Calais with the refugees, there were also a great many French Fifth Columnists, and we were now forced to treat everyone not wearing a British uniform as a potential enemy. It was a situation that had its tragic aspects, for in some places French and Belgian troops were fighting bravely by the side of the British.

But what interested us most was some very secret inside information that a number of soldiers were only too willing to impart to us. The Canadians were landing in force tomorrow, and reinforcements were also coming from Dunkirk. Within the next two days more and more troops would pour into Calais, and once they arrived we, the advance guard, would be evacuated.

At first we were inclined to disbelieve all these stories, but when we came to halt at the embarkation point and were told to fall out and wait for further orders, we were finally convinced that what we had been told was true. Obviously, things were already moving in the direction of our evacuation. The way matters were going it seemed that we might even be taken off that night. It was all very encouraging. Settling comfortably in the grass, I scrounged a cigarette and relaxed. Already I could see myself arriving at Dover, going on leave, and holding forth in the local pubs to an appreciative audience with all the authority of a battle-seasoned soldier.

Night fell and we were still waiting, with the red glow of the sky behind us lit from time to time by the white flashes of the German artillery. We had been there for some hours when a warship finally arrived. Looming out of the darkness it bore gently down on the quay, the most solid and reassuring thing we had seen for days. There was no doubt about it now. We were really going home. Already everyone was on their feet, waiting impatiently to feel the gangplank beneath them.

But surprisingly enough no one seemed in any hurry to

get us on board. The ship slid silently in against the quay, a gangplank was lowered, and for a while there seemed to be rather a lot of coming and going up and down it. But for some reason or other no one took any notice of us standing there, waiting to go on board.

The brutal truth was finally broken to us by a Sergeant who came up from the quay and was immediately surrounded by a throng of men thirsting for information.

'What's happening, Sarge?'

'What time do we go on board, Sarge?'

'We're not waiting for the others, are we, Sarge?'

The Sergeant looked around him. 'No one's going on board,' he said quietly. 'The ship's brought us more ammunition to keep us going, that's all.'

Worse was to follow. As we sank to the ground in stunned silence, an officer came bustling up.

'On your feet, men,' he said tersely.

Quickly we gathered around him. Perhaps they had changed their minds. Perhaps we were going to be evacuated after all.

'Are we going aboard now, sir?' someone asked.

'No, we're not!' the officer said grimly. 'Not now or tomorrow or ever! We're staying here to the end. Now get yourselves sorted out into your platoons. We're making a counter-attack!'

I looked at the ship, and then turned and looked at the blazing inferno of the town we were about to enter. Suddenly I felt very tired. I stood there for some time looking at it, and then someone dug me in the ribs and I found myself stumbling along with the platoon, away from the quay and the ship and all immediate hopes of getting home.

We walked for some time, and then came to a halt beside a high wall. A sudden burst of Bren-gun fire ahead told us that another platoon had made contact with the enemy.

'What's happening, sir?' someone asked the officer leading the platoon.

'We're staying here as reserve,' he said.

'Did you hear that?' the rifleman beside me said excitedly. 'We're staying right here. Maybe we won't be needed.'

'Oh, balls to the lot of it,' I said wearily. And leaning against the wall, I fell asleep.

When I awoke again the noise of the battle had died down, except for an occasional burst from a Bren gun and some spasmodic rifle fire. Soon after that it ceased altogether.

The next day the Germans settled down in earnest to the task of destroying Calais and everyone in it. Soon after dawn, artillery and mortar fire poured steadily into the town and the dock area. Fortunately, by that time we had left our positions of the night before, and had dug ourselves in along the bank of the basin, together with some other platoons who had also gravitated to the same spot.

With four men to each fox-hole, we sat and waited quietly for trouble. We did not have long to wait. Later that morning, the first Stukas arrived, flying in steady formation almost directly above us. Below, we tried to make ourselves as small as possible in our holes, and a few moments later the first bombs dropped, sending great cascades of earth spouting up in the air around us. After that the Stukas kept coming, wave after wave of them, and each time they came the four of us fought for the lowest place in the hole, counted the thuds as the bombs dropped, and between breaths cursed the British Air Force for not being around. In one of the brief intervals, a Sergeant ran along the bank dropping packets of Woodbines into the fox-holes. He had hardly got back to his own hole, when the planes were over again.

It was a British warship which helped to give us a much-needed respite. Arriving in the middle of a raid, it brought the four of us out from the bottom of our hole to watch the warship's pom-pom guns pumping shells among the Stukas droning above us. Watching the flaming balls of fire streaking across the sky, we forgot the bombs dropping around us and joined in the cheering coming from the other fox-holes along the bank. A Stuka dived towards the sea enveloped in flames. The rest flew on until we could see them no more.

Although the Stukas didn't come over again after that, the four of us in that hole had only a brief respite before we were in trouble once more. We were still puffing furiously at our first cigarettes, trying to calm our nerves and adjust ourselves to the sudden silence, when a Sergeant loomed up on the edge of the hole.

'All right, you four,' he barked. 'Out of there, and make it quick!'

As we quickly scrambled out of the hole, we saw there were four other riflemen standing behind the Sergeant. They did not look very happy.

'What's up, Sarge?' I asked.

'German troops have been seen entering a factory near here,' he said crisply. 'And we're going in to get them!'

'Oh,' I said. I could understand now why those four riflemen looked so miserable.

As we followed the Sergeant along the bank, a rifleman popped his head up from one of the holes.

'You chaps going to get us some grub?' he asked hopefully.

'You've got a hope,' I said. 'We're just off to get ourselves killed in a raid. Want to come along?'

'Christ!' the rifleman said, quickly disappearing from sight.

It seemed ages before we reached the factory, which turned out to be a great, gaunt-looking building surrounded by a high wall. Quickly we slipped through the gates and ran silently for the shelter of the time-keeper's office. Peering cautiously around it, I looked at the vast yard and then at the windows of the factory. There were hundreds of windows, enough places for a whole German regiment to take up positions and train their guns on that yard which we had to cross. The thought of sprinting across it under those windows was a very depressing one.

'We're going to make a dash for it,' the Sergeant whispered, pointing to a door at the far end of the yard. 'Once we're inside . . .' The shrill scream of a mortar bomb sailing towards us interrupted him.

'Out!' the Sergeant roared.

As we began running for the gates, the first bomb landed in the middle of the yard. The next moment I was outside, taking a flying dive for cover beneath the inevitable lorry that always seemed to be standing around whenever there was trouble of this sort. Lying curled up under it, I watched the legs of some of the others as they ran past the truck. Then there was a scream of a mortar bomb again, and suddenly a portion of the factory wall was no longer there, only bricks spraying out fanwise and a great cloud of dust and black smoke that billowed forward and enveloped everything.

As I lay under the truck, choking and blinded, I heard the sound of the mortar again and the bomb drop nearby. After that there was only silence. Gradually the smoke cleared, and in front of me, almost in line with the lorry, I saw the bodies of two riflemen lying motionless and bloody amid the rubble. After a suitable interval I scrambled up from beneath the truck and began to run, expecting to hear the silence broken by a mortar bomb pursuing me. But the hidden mortar gun remained silent.

Some time later I was still running, thinking it rather strange that I had not caught up with any of the others, and becoming conscious of the fact that the scenery seemed rather unfamiliar. I came to an abrupt halt, and looked around in sudden panic, conscious that I was lost and with no idea where I was beyond the fact that I was standing in the middle of a narrow footpath that wound along beside a high bank that stretched along the whole length of the path. Faintly I could hear the sound of the sea coming from over the other side of the bank.

I began walking slowly, acutely conscious that for all I knew of the positions I could be walking straight into the hands of the Germans. To add to everything, a mortar opened up. The bomb burst on the bank some yards behind me, and once more I was galloping along the path.

The mortar kept thudding, the bombs kept screaming over my head, and I kept running, convinced that it would now be only a matter of seconds before I was hit.

Farther along I saw the reason for the concentrated mortar fire. Heads poking cautiously out of fox-holes as I ran on down the path told me that I had stumbled on one of our positions. At that moment, however, it was not much help to me. They were all single fox-holes, and I felt that my arrival and the resultant congestion would not make me very popular.

What finally brought me to a halt was the sight of three soldiers sitting unconcernedly out in the open near the footpath. Quite oblivious to the noise and the bombs falling around them, they squatted over a small twig fire, watching a mess-tin containing some dark-brown liquid coming to the boil. As I joined them I could see that they were obviously Regulars, real old sweats, who must have almost done their time when the war had started, pinning them down for further service. They were also three of the roughest and toughest-looking men I had ever seen.

'Just in time for a cup of tea,' one of them said cheerfully. He was a squat little man with cauliflower ears and was wearing Corporal's stripes. The other two looked up briefly, nodded, and then turned their attention to the mess-tin again.

A mortar bomb exploded and I winced.

'Forget it, Charlie boy,' the Corporal said. 'We've all had it, anyway. No reason, though, why we shouldn't have a nice cuppa char before we go, is there?'

The mess-tin was boiling now. One of the soldiers picked up a tin of condensed milk that lay beside him and, stabbing it with his bayonet, poured some into the mess-tin. Stirring it with a grubby finger, he politely passed me the mess-tin.

'After you, mate,' he said.

I took two great gulps of tea. It tasted wonderful. At that moment another mortar bomb exploded, perilously near this time. 'Thanks for the tea,' I said, looking at the great clod of earth that had landed within a few feet of us, 'but I think I'd better be on my way.'

'Where do you think you're going, anyway?' the Corporal asked. He listened sympathetically while I told him what had happened. When I finished he said: 'Why don't you stay with us, son? No sense in running off your backside for nothing. Everything is in such a bloody shambles now that it doesn't make much difference where you are.'

For a moment I was tempted. But the sound of another mortar bomb made me realize that I was not really resigned enough to sit around in the open and wait for something to drop on me.

'Thanks,' I said, 'but I think I'd like to get back to my platoon.'

'Take one of these with you, chum,' one of the soldiers said, holding out a cigarette packet. Seeing there were only two in it, I hesitated. Impatiently he pulled one out and stuck it behind my ear.

'Thanks,' I said again. And then I was on my way.

Behind me, the three Regulars were busily preparing another brew.

I continued down the path, and then miraculously the scenery seemed familiar once more and I knew that I had come out on the edge of the basin again. Soon afterwards, I was running happily towards my fox-hole.

We remained in our holes all day, listening to the noise of the battle raging in the town growing louder and louder with every passing hour. Occasionally the Stukas came over, dropped their bombs, and then flew off, always without opposition. Not once did we see a British plane. It was just one more thing to add to the growing feeling that we had been sacrificed for nothing. The very absence of planes seemed to indicate that Calais itself was no longer important, and we were therefore only indulging in futile heroics. If someone had once bothered to tell us that our presence in Calais was helping the B.E.F. in their escape from France, it would have made all the difference.

Darkness came and the noise of battle in the town died down, until in the end there was only the sound of Calais burning. Soon afterwards we received the order to move and slipping quietly out of our holes we made our way swiftly towards the *Gare Maritime*. On the way we heard rumours of evacuation. There was a possibility of an eventual withdrawal to the beach, where the Navy would come in and take us off. Once more there was hope.

At dawn the German artillery opened up, and shells began to fall around the *Gare Maritime*, shattering the windows of the station and setting alight a string of cattle trucks that stood in the marshalling yard. After that the Stukas came over, bombing and machine-gunning the quays. In the brief intervals between the shell fire and the Stuka raids, troops wandered aimlessly around the station and dock area, waiting for further orders. But organized resistance was already over.

Soon afterwards an order did come through. It was now every man for himself. There was no longer any talk of being evacuated by the Navy. The end was very near, and we were stuck with it; the burning town, the almost non-stop dive-bombing from the Stukas; the tanks and the troops approaching us—and the empty sea behind us. We knew then that the best we could hope for was being taken prisoner-of-war.

CHAPTER TWO

For You the War is Over

THE hour before the end should have been the worst part of it all, but surprisingly enough it wasn't. The shells had been coming over even more frequently than before, still dropping mostly around the *Gare Maritime* goods yard and along the *Bassin de Chasses*, and with some success, for the area was littered with dead bodies. But now there were no more illusions as to our future and the only thing to do was to make the best of it, an almost ebullient gaiety had begun to enliven the proceedings. Joking loudly among themselves, troops began to settle down among the rubble and along the side of the basin to make a last stand. Everyone suddenly seemed in very good spirits, and doing my best to enter into the general mood I tilted my helmet rakishly on one side and went off to see if I could find some of my platoon, so that I could at least die or go into captivity among friends.

Somehow or other I landed up on the railway station, where I found a number of British troops, more concerned with finishing off the wine in the bar than with the shells falling around the station. Unfortunately, by the time I arrived most of the wine had gone, and as there seemed no point in staying, I went out on to the platform again and made my way towards a small fort I could see on the coast.

I found the fort occupied by a number of troops and two officers. As I arrived, one of the officers was busily haranguing the troops on the need for discipline in this final hour. Some of the men had also made their way from the station, and it was evident that they had been far luckier than I had in getting to the wine casks.

The sudden bang of a mortar shell landing near the fort silenced the officer. There were more bangs, and we knew then that it had not just been a chance shell that had landed near us. The Germans had arrived.

The fort was nothing more than a glorified pill-box, and the only way we could effectively defend it was by getting out of it and taking up positions on a high bank a few yards in front of it. We made our last stand on that bank, and the rest is lost to me in the haze of concentration of the brief battle. Only fragments remain—tracer shells screaming over our heads, bullets thudding into the soft earth around us; an officer vainly signalling to a fishing-boat in the calm waters beyond; brief whispered words of reassurance to the dying turning grey, even as we looked into their faces and tried to smile encouragingly. And then the end. A white flag was hoisted, and a few minutes later we were advancing towards the Germans with our hands in the air.

It is a little difficult to say what my precise feelings were at that time. Relief, I suppose. Relief that I was one of the more lucky ones, and not one of the many dead that lay around Calais.

It had been a short action, lasting only five days, and it was really rather surprising that it had lasted as long as that. About four thousand of us had managed to hold the town against two Panzer regiments who had skirmished in and around Calais for days before deciding to come in for the final blow. The German Intelligence must have been pretty poor, especially as the whole town had been riddled with Fifth Columnists.

After having been searched for weapons, we were taken to a large field where a great number of prisoners were already sitting on the grass, looking rather frightened and miserable. Soon after we had joined them, the Navy came on the scene and began shelling the town.

We sat there for a long time, waiting for something to happen, but nothing did, except that more prisoners joined us as the hours went by.

Late that afternoon one of our officers came over and told us that he had a message for us all from the Kommandant.

The Kommandant stood close behind him, smiling pleasantly, revealing a rather fine set of gold teeth. We glowered back at the Kommandant, and made no move to get up. The Kommandant's smile became a little fixed. The officer then launched on his speech on behalf of the Kommandant, which, as it turned out, was a complimentary and gracious one of the 'valiant foes' and 'magnificent defence' variety. After it was over, the British officer and the Kommandant shook hands. It was rather silly of us, I suppose, but we rather perked up at that speech. For one thing, it did make us look at the business of being a prisoner-of-war in a different light. It made it less humiliating, and rather more as if we were on the side of a defeated cricket team, hearing the cries of 'bad luck, sir' before going in for tea and crumpets.

After that there was more waiting. The sun went down, a faint breeze sprang up, and depression settled upon us again. As I stood there puffing at a cigarette, I watched our officers, who stood in a rather self-conscious group, slightly apart from us. I've no doubt in a way they felt even worse than we did, probably thinking that we were blaming them for getting us into this hole. I am sorry to say that, very unfairly, most of us were.

The Navy stopped shelling the town almost at the same moment as we were given the order to move. We got to our feet, straggled out on to the road, and were then told to start marching. Keeping close together for protection, we began walking down the road towards the town.

Going through the town of Calais was a humiliating experience. As we marched through the streets, people emerged from their houses and shops and stood watching us with cold, almost hostile eyes, as we stumbled past them over the cobbled roads. Not one of them spoke or even smiled. Suddenly, I had the feeling that was to become common to a lot of prisoners whenever they were watched by civilians—the feeling that one was no longer looked upon as a human being who had once had a life of his own, but merely as something abstract that was only categorized as a

British, French, or Russian prisoner. If a uniform makes one anonymous, the brand of prisoner-of-war carries one a stage further.

On the outskirts of the town we began to come across the bodies of our troops who had fought a rear-guard action there. A Rifle Brigade soldier, flopped over his Bren gun, his eyeballs hanging on his cheeks, watched us pass. One man who was still alive, his leg shattered from the knee downwards, cried for water as we passed, and was ignored by the German guards, who went by as if he was not there.

Outside the town, I was suddenly aware of a sweet, sickly smell in the air. Soon afterwards we passed a railway siding full of open, shattered cattle trucks, and I saw that the smell was coming from the dead horses, whose bloated bodies filled the trucks and spilled out on to the tracks. This smell of death was to be with us often during the early days of the march, coming not from horses but from the dead that still lay in the fields.

We were very tired that evening as we walked along the quiet country roads. No one spoke much, except a Sergeant who was talking *all* the time, busily giving us instructions on how to escape and link up with the British forces when they crossed our path. That was how much we knew about Dunkirk.

We marched until it was dark. And then, suddenly, a halt was called outside a church. A few seconds later we were pushed in among the graves and told that this was our resting-place for the night. I remember thinking that this was probably the German idea of a joke. After that I laid down on a tombstone and watched the glow of a guard's cigarette as he paced up and down outside the cemetery. Although someone had their boot in my face, I was asleep in a matter of minutes.

The next day we had a new set of guards. They were members of the *Toten Kopf*—Death's Head Panzer Corps, with a silver skull as their insignia; and as soon as they took over, we knew that the make-believe that had been enacted between the German Kommandant and our officers at Calais was over. Maybe it was because we were all a little cowed by the events of the last few days, but most of them seemed hulking great fellows, very impressive in their jack-boots and black uniforms. They were swaggering, arrogant, and flamboyant, and personified to the life Hitler's new race of *Herrenvolk*. Nearly all of them carried rubber trun-cheons, which they used on the slightest pretext. If a man wandered slightly out of the column, or stumbled, or was not moving fast enough, one of the Panzer troopers would be on him, belting him around the head with a fine dis-regard for his skull.

Most of the time the Panzer Corps guards set us a fast pace along the roads, and it was not easy for us to keep up. We had scarcely had time to eat at Calais, and we had cer-tainly not eaten since we had been captured. What was more, we did not see much chance of getting fed in the near future or any other time. The Panzer boys seemed more in a mood to finish us off rather than keep us alive.

Those in the rear of the column—my usual place—were particularly unfortunate. With fewer men to hide among, one was more vulnerable there. Consequently, whenever the guards in the rear started on us, we would indirectly set the whole column into a panic. With someone laying into you with all his might, the only thing to do was to try to push through the others in front of you. As soon as we tried to go forward, those in front would also begin to run rather than be caught up in the trouble behind them. This running spread through the whole column, until in the end we were all stumbling along the road as fast as our legs could carry us. By that time other guards had joined in the sport, and were also joyfully helping us along with their truncheons.

It was not long before the guards thought up another delightful pastime to while away the boring hours on the road. On the front and rear of the column was a truck with a machine-gun on it. Both these guns pointed over our heads, ready to catch us in a fore-and-aft fire if necessary.

Whenever the gunner at the front of the column felt like it, he would let fly across our heads. As we dived to the ground, the truck in the rear would immediately begin to accelerate, with the result that we had to spring to our feet again and run like mad to get out of the way. The Panzer boys thought this a huge joke and repeated it frequently.

To add to our troubles, we had visits from high-spirited Luftwaffe pilots, who swooped low over the column, sending us diving for the ditches. I cannot say that the Panzer boys enjoyed this either, as they, too, had to make a dive for it.

Fortunately, the *Toten Kopf* guards were not with us for long. We were handed over to another set of guards, and things quietened down a little. By that time, however, we had begun to wonder when we were going to be fed and put on a train for Germany. Most of us had existed so far on rations left over from Calais, or from a few potatoes dug up out of the fields and baked among the twigs we were able to find in the fields in which we stopped for the night. As for the train—no one imagined for a moment that there was going to be no train.

During the whole of that march, the guards kept telling us that a train was nearby; always at the next town or village. Later, when we made it clear that we had got tired of that story, it was three days' march to the nearest railway junction that could cope with so many prisoners. But, in the meantime: 'Keep marching, *Kamerad*. You have nothing to worry about. For you the war is over.'

And yet, despite all this, we never quite gave up hope that one day we really would see that train that would put an end to the marching and starvation.

The food problem was becoming worse every day. The German rations for prisoners were almost non-existent. Very occasionally there was a soup issue, which looked like greasy water, and had one or two small pieces of potato floating in it. Sometimes there was also an issue of a small piece of German rye bread, green with mould. As more and more French, Belgian, and British prisoners converged on the column, it was quite common to reach the field-kitchens to find nothing left. It was on this sort of diet that we were expected to march between twenty and thirty miles a day.

To live at all, we had to find food the best way we could. The fields helped us a little, but it was not very easy to get into them. The Germans at that time were adopting a policy of behaving correctly towards the French. This meant that whenever one dived into a field in search of potatoes or mangel-wurzels, one was generally booted out of it by some guard making a great display of protecting French property. Actually, during that march the Germans did everything they could to play the French against the British. They did not have to try very hard.

It was fortunate that it was a hot summer that year. Most nights we slept in the fields, waking at dawn to find ourselves covered with dew. Nearly all of us had lost our blankets, gas-capes, and ground-sheets, which had been taken off us at some time or another by the German guards. Despite their good equipment, they seemed short of such things. On the few occasions we did go under cover for the night, the conditions were so dreadful that we would have gladly spent the night outside in the pouring rain.

The night at Doullens was a typical example. Arriving there one sweltering afternoon, we were all put into the local prison, and packed so tight in it that each cell overflowed its occupants on to the landings and down the stairs, which were blocked solid. There was not one place in the whole prison where a man could lie down, and if anyone wanted to relieve himself he was forced to do so where he stood. I shared a cell with Senegalese troops, who were far more philosophical about the conditions than I was.

Soon after that we began entering villages more often. German troops were billeted in many of them, and invariably they would come out of the houses and line the road to watch us pass. On these occasions they stood and jeered at us, while the Germans who wanted souvenirs would dart forward and snatch a watch or a tin helmet from a prisoner.

The guards did not bother to interfere. The favourite joke among the Germans was to bawl out Winston Churchill's name and then go into a violent pantomime demonstrating him being hanged. We replied with a slightly different version of Winston's 'V' sign.

Every time we reached a village not occupied by the Germans, the column suddenly went into action. Ignoring the guards, everyone broke column and headed at full pelt for the shops and houses. A few minutes later, the shop-owners were on the pavements, yelling for the guards. The prisoners meanwhile were frantically pilfering everything in sight. Others were busy grubbing for vegetables in the gardens or knocking at the doors for food. The general technique was to point to one's mouth and rattle off all the French words one knew for food. Very undignified, but sometimes effective.

My first attempts at this sort of thing were not very successful. Knocking at a door, I politely lifted my helmet to the woman who came to it. Before she had time to slam the door in my face, I quickly inserted my foot and rattled off the established formula: *'Avez-vous du pain? Du beurre? Confiture? Des œufs?'* The woman went away, and a few seconds later returned with a brown-paper parcel. I lifted my helmet and retreated, congratulating myself on my personal charm. After I had gone a few yards down the road, I opened the packet, to find that all it contained was an old pair of women's shoes.

While all this sort of thing was going on, the place was in an uproar. Screaming guards pursued prisoners; the villagers yelled abuse, and to add to the din, more often than not fights broke out between the French and British prisoners. From time to time a prisoner was unfortunate enough to get a bullet in his leg or a bayonet dug up his rear. But by now there were so many of us that each man considered that the odds were so much in his favour that it was worth taking a chance. I found these sorties really quite exciting. In the wild scramble for food, I forgot that I was tired, that I had been walking since dawn, and that I was very, very hungry.

The more enterprising prisoners were sometimes able to steal a chicken or a rabbit, and it soon became an almost common sight to see a British prisoner grimly pursuing a squawking chicken, with the enraged owner close behind and a frantic guard in fourth place. The Germans were rather humourless about it all. I remember seeing a German guard screaming with fury as he chased a prisoner along the road, beating him over the head with a dead rabbit which he had snatched from the prisoner's hands.

None of us had any false pride in begging for food. The situation was far too desperate for that. But there was not much in the villages. There were eggs, which we punctured and sucked; a little butter which one ate off one's fingers in great solid blobs, a little bread, and a few biscuits and fruit. It was these things that kept us going, certainly not the German rations. There were also a number of villages where we did not have the heart to try anything—villages in ruins, the only inhabitants a few stony-faced peasants who watched us pass as if we were not there and they were not even looking.

Every so often someone would fall out by the roadside, unable to carry on any longer. They would lie there, almost indifferent to the kicks and blows that the guards showered on them. I do not know what happened to them. All I know is that I never saw any transport bringing them up later, and this in itself seemed a very good reason to keep going at all costs. Collectively, one was fairly safe—lost in the mob. Alone, it was rather a different matter; anything could happen.

Sometimes we would come across a portion of the road littered with torn documents, French helmets, and overturned tanks, and then we would get the smell of death in our nostrils again. Occasionally we would see a rough wooden cross with a German helmet stuck on top of it.

After a while, I teamed up with a couple of Cockneys, Albert and Charlie, and between us we worked out an almost infallible method of getting food from the villagers. Charlie, who had a rather delicate and battered look not in keeping with his constitution, would hang limply between Albert and myself, his arms around our necks. We would then drag him to a front door, ring the bell, and as soon as the house owner came, fix him with a reproachful eye. Charlie would then groan in the most heart-rending manner, and roll his eyeballs, as if on the point of dying. Rather than be asked to give shelter to a dying prisoner, the householder would scamper off and return a few seconds later with some food. One could almost see the relief in their eyes as we moved off, with Charlie still groaning. Unfortunately, the performance was sometimes spoilt by the arrival of a guard in the middle of it all. The house owners must have been very surprised at Charlie's rapid recovery as the three of us sped down the road at top speed.

Sometimes, on the more desolate stretches of the road, I would think about what lay before us in Germany. My impressions of prisoner-of-war life were somewhat hazy. One or two of the guards had told us that we would go out on working parties, probably on farms. Others, with great glee, informed us that we would undoubtedly end up in the mines, doing sixteen hours a day. That prospect was too alarming to think about, so instead, I would think of myself on one of those farms, not doing too much work, and probably with a room of my own, where I could do a little light reading in the evenings; by some miraculous means I was suddenly able to read fluently in German. Probably, I also thought, there might be some farm wench on hand to help me pass the time. As I said, my impressions of prisoner-of-war life were more than a little hazy. I was due for a rude awakening.

When we reached Cambrai, the first rumours began and spread down the column like wildfire. The English were counter-attacking and the Germans retreating. Next—the British had made tremendous gains. After that the British were quite near—rescue was at hand. These rumours were so eagerly accepted that someone was sure they had heard guns in the night. Those strange, impossible rumours, coming from God knows where, pursued us in one form or another for the rest of our days as prisoners-of-war. The amazing thing was that one never entirely ceased to believe in them.

We stayed several days at Cambrai, living and sleeping on the enormous parade-ground of the local barracks. During that time there was only one issue of bread and soup, enough for perhaps a quarter of the men there. Then, as usual, supplies ran out, and, as usual, we starved. However, we did have those rumours to keep us going. We believed in the rumours so much that when the time came for us to leave, most of us were still looking over our shoulders, almost as if we expected to see the British Army charging down the road behind us. We were not simple-minded. We just wanted to believe in something that would help us through the day. Tomorrow there might be something else to keep us going—that train that would take us to Germany, a loaf of bread, or even a single cigarette.

By this time the bad feeling between the British and French prisoners had reached a point where both sides hated each other only slightly less than they did their captors. The French resented the idea of us robbing their soil and pushing into the houses, where they considered they had first claim, and we, who had been in Calais, could not forget what had happened there. The rest of the British disliked them because the few villagers who were in the position to hand out food gave it to the French rather than to us.

All this would have been bad enough if it had ended there. But now there was also a great deal of animosity among ourselves. The column had begun to split up into little bands, combines as they called them, each in fierce competition with the other for food. At one time the individual on the road had been philosophic, or at the most mildly irritated, whenever he had been beaten to a house where there was food. With the setting up of the combines, each of them with a self-elected leader, the foraging for food became a deadly business, leading to continual fights in which the weakest always went to the wall, and therefore starved for most of the march. Everybody was against everybody, with fights and petty thieving going on all the time. At night, one hardly dared sleep because of the night prowlers who crawled around the field, trying to steal your gas-mask container in the hope that it might contain cigarettes or a few scraps of bread.

As far as Charlie, Albert, and I were concerned, the road from Cambrai was not a very happy one. We had not eaten for several days, and we were so weak from hunger that it was as much as we could do to drag ourselves along the road. It did not stop us from quarrelling, however. Each suddenly began to accuse the others of not having done their fair share of the scrounging, and the recriminations went on for miles, as we hurled abuse at each other and swore that we would break up the partnership at the next stop.

During the whole of that day we did not go through one village, and to add to everything I lost my tin helmet to a German soldier seeking a souvenir. This was a grave loss, as it had been my soup-bowl, wash-bowl, and head covering combined. Now that I had no helmet, I had nothing in which to collect soup whenever it was dished out.

We finally staggered into Valenciennes in the early hours of the morning, after the longest and toughest day on the road to date. We reckoned that we had covered the best part of forty miles.

At that moment, when it just did not seem worth trying to go on any longer, something happened. As we came into town at the tail end of the column, we suddenly heard a whisper from a doorway. Scenting food, we made a mad rush. We found an elderly German soldier standing there, a loaf of bread under his arm. Looking cautiously down the road, he quickly tore the loaf into three pieces and stuffed them into our hands. The next moment he was pushing us gently out into the road again. We were so staggered that we did not even argue about who should have the largest piece.

Dawn was breaking when we finally collapsed in a field on the other side of Valenciennes. All around us lay the ghostly sleeping figures of those who had arrived there hours before us.

About eleven o'clock the next morning we set off again and began to head for Mons. At first it looked as if we were in for another bad day. Then we had a stroke of luck. Coming across a deserted farmhouse, we scuttled past the guard and investigated the yard, where we found an egg vat with about two dozen eggs in it.

Having decided to keep the eggs until the evening, we carried them in our gas-mask containers until we reached our usual nightly field. We then settled down for our meal. Albert broke the eggs one by one into his helmet, stirred them vigorously with his fingers, and then added a little sugar which he had produced unexpectedly from his pocket. We looked at him accusingly, and Albert quickly explained that he had merely been keeping it for such an emergency as this. The helmet then went the rounds. That egg-nog was the best meal we had had on the march so far.

The next day we reached Waterloo, and here for the first time we had a full-scale demonstration of sympathy. As soon as we came into the main street, cigarette packets by the dozen began to drop from the passing trams, shop-keepers ran out with tins of food or whatever was available, while farther down the road a baker threw loaf after loaf out on to the pavement. In the matter of a few minutes the whole street was filled with prisoners fighting over the food and cigarettes, yelling guards going for the prisoners and civilians, and stationary trams joyously clanging their bells to add to the general din. Finally, however, the guards' rifle-butts began to take effect, and the column moved on out of the town.

A few days later we reached the Dutch border town of Maastricht, and we were all crammed into a small field some way outside the town. To our amazement, a German medical officer suddenly made an appearance. A tent was put up for him, and a little later he was busy dealing with the long queues waiting to see him. Despite the fact that there had been a number of walking wounded on the march, this was the first time that medical treatment had been provided.

The column set off again early the next morning, leaving behind the unfit, who were being taken the rest of the way in lorries. We were all joined up later in the day in another field. But this was a very different field from the others. A railway track ran beside it. No sooner had the last prisoner appeared in the field than a train appeared, pulling behind it a long line of cattle trucks. For an awful moment I thought it was going to pass us without stopping. But instead it halted suddenly, and the cattle trucks slowly buffeted to a stop in front of us.

A cheer rang out across the field. Everyone began to walk towards the trucks, quite slowly at first, as if they were still not really sure that the trucks were intended for them. It was not until they saw the guards pulling open the doors that everyone began to run. As each man was counted off and allocated to a truck, he was given a third of a loaf of bread and a small piece of sausage.

When the door was finally closed on the truck I was in, I found there were nearly eighty men in it, so there was only room for a few of us to sit down. The rest had to stand in one spot, barely able to move a foot.

And so we crossed the border into Germany. I was not to return until five years later.

CHAPTER THREE

Stalag VIIIB

WE had entered the trucks grateful that our walking days were over. We would have perhaps been less grateful if we had known that we were to spend three days in those trucks before reaching our destination.

The first few hours passed pleasantly enough, and Charlie, Albert, and I spent them standing by one of the windows, looking at the passing countryside while we nibbled cautiously at our bread and sausage. Despite the crowded conditions of the truck, the stifling heat, and the meagre rations for the journey, the general conversation around us reflected a growing optimism hardly justified by our treatment so far.

Just before dark the train stopped and we were let out to relieve ourselves. After that the train did not stop again until well into the early hours of the morning, when it finally ground to a halt just outside a main station. Faintly we could hear the voice of the station announcer, his voice an unintelligible blur as it came through the loudspeakers. Then the long line of cattle trucks began moving again, and after a complicated series of shuntings backwards and forwards, came to a halt in a large marshalling yard just outside the station.

For a long time I stood by the window, looking at the changing signals and the trains flashing by on the main line. Then there were no more passenger trains, only an occasional goods train that shunted past with clinking couplings, and then came to a halt, its trucks buffeting together in a series of loud bangs that echoed hollowly around the yard.

Squatting on the floor at my feet, Charlie and Albert discussed our prospects for the future.

'Army grub without the trimmings,' Charlie said, 'that's what we'll get.'

'We might even be sent out to work on a farm,' Albert said. 'That'll mean eggs, bacon, milk—the lot. Maybe it won't be so bad, after all.'

'We might even get ourselves a bit of "grumble" if we go out to work,' Charlie said thoughtfully.

They were still discussing that happy possibility when I slid to the floor beside them.

'German girls are hot stuff,' Charlie was saying. 'I knew a bloke who ...'

The experiences of Charlie's friend were lost to me, for at that moment I went to sleep.

Soon after dawn we moved again. Travelling very slowly, the train passed field after field of barley and corn, an occasional village, and then more fields, countless acres of fields. But as the day wore on, the stifling heat inside the truck, cramp pains, and filling bladders gave us something more than the scenery to think about. By the late afternoon we were gritting our teeth and trying to assure ourselves that at any moment now the train would stop and we would be let out to relieve ourselves. But the train did not stop. Instead it went on and on, hour after hour, until in the end we gave up trying to be civilized. By the evening the truck smelt worse than a French urinal.

The train went on all through the night and half the following day before it finally stopped again. The doors of the truck slid open, and we swarmed out and joined the solid mass of men moving on the fields like an advancing army. After a brief period of ecstatic relief in the grass, we were marching quite happily, if a little unsteadily, through some rather pleasant countryside on our way to the camp. The worst was now over. No more marching, no more sleeping in fields, no more travelling in cattle trucks; instead, an organized camp life, regular rations, and nothing to do but wait for the end.

The camp, unfortunately, was a distinct let-down, consisting of nothing more than several enormous marquees standing in the middle of a field and surrounded by barbed wire. The Kommandant, a middle-aged, rather distinguished-looking man, stood at the gate to greet us. As the first of us passed him, filthy, unshaven, and smelling to high heaven, his nostrils wrinkled with distaste.

'Filthy English swine,' he said distinctly.

We marched past him with as much dignity as we could muster under the circumstances. As we made for the tents, it struck me that 'waiting for the end' was going to entail a little more hardship than we had anticipated.

But even so, we were grateful for the doubtful comforts that the camp had to offer us. A bed of straw and a roof of sorts was a distinct improvement on the past few weeks, and even if the bowl of soup and piece of bread that we received daily was somewhat less than our first wild expectations, there was still the consolation of being able to rest, with the knowledge that we would still be in the camp the following day, and not walking along some dusty road that stretched on without end.

But as the days went by, hunger and boredom took over, and suddenly those weeks on the march no longer seemed quite so terrible. During that period there had at least been a chance to get more food than we were getting now, and the concentration and energy required to get it had left little time for brooding on the future. Now there was all the time in the world to think, and the more we thought the less we liked the look of things. A special parade, with the Kommandant exultantly informing us of France's capitulation and the evacuation of the B.E.F., plunged us into even deeper despair.

Fortunately, as far as the camp itself was concerned, our fears for the future were unfounded. It turned out that it was only a transit camp, and soon after the Kommandant's depressing news, we were out of it, travelling in cattle trucks towards our final destination. Several days later we entered Stalag VIIIB.

Stalag VIIIB stood outside a small village called Lamsdorf, in Upper Silesia, and was to become the largest prisoner-of-war camp in Germany; a self-contained world of its own, with a steady population of ten thousand men, plus a float of roughly two hundred men who had escaped from the *Strafe* compound at one time or another, and then quietly lost themselves among the rest. When we arrived, however, Stalag VIIIB had not come into its own, and housed only a handful of prisoners—soldiers taken in Norway, a few R.A.F. personnel, some merchant seamen, and a number of Poles who were kept in a separate compound.

On entering Stalag VIIIB, we were impressed by its well-laid-out appearance and the almost new barracks, with their double-tiered bunks and comfortable-looking straw mattresses. There were latrines that were not too odorous, and, most welcome sight of all, a large kitchen, where men could be seen busy over huge vats of steaming soup. But despite the air of being well organized, Stalag VIIIB soon proved to be no holiday camp. No provision had been made to deal with the thousands of prisoners that had suddenly poured into it, and within the space of a week or so the beds were full of bugs and the pits beneath the latrines filling rapidly and smelling abominably. The prisoners themselves were lice-ridden, without medical attention, and existing on a daily diet that consisted of a ladleful of soup, two or three rotten potatoes, and a third of a loaf between three men.

The soup that came up each day contained a few small bones, some vegetable stalks, a shred or two of meat, and an occasional potato. Although it never varied, it was sent up by the kitchen under a variety of names. On Monday it was vegetable soup; Tuesday—potato soup; Wednesday—carrot soup; Thursday—bone soup; Friday—beetroot soup; Saturday and Sunday—goulash stew. Whatever failings the kitchen staff might have had, they did not lack imagination.

The bread ration was the only thing that really kept us going. Under the circumstances, it was not surprising that the daily division of a third of a loaf between three men was carried out under some stress and with a fanatical insistence on the part of everyone for his rightful share down to the last crumb. The division of the bread was a fairly lengthy operation, carried out in several stages. First, there was the marking off of the three portions, checked time and time again, just in case the first measurements were a fraction out. The loaf was then sawn through very slowly and with careful regard that the knife did not deviate by a fraction in its downward cut. The three portions were then measured one against the other, examined individually to see if there was any loss in one portion through a sloping crust, and then finally laid down on the table. To discourage any subtle skulduggery with the knife, the cutter always took the last portion left on the table.

After we had been there about a week, the Germans got down to the business of registering us as prisoners-of-war. Everyone was shaven to the skull, photographed, finger-printed, and then given a registration number and disc; also a postcard to write home. After all this, those whose clothes were in rags were marched down to the stores and surrendered to a bad-tempered little German private, who seemed to resent bitterly our intrusion on his privacy. After much screaming on the part of the storekeeper and some frantic undressing and dressing on my part, I emerged, dressed in a pair of French cavalry trousers several sizes too large, a Polish forage-cap several sizes too small, a Belgian jacket that had a suspicious hole in it just above the heart, and a pair of enormous Dutch wooden clogs. Socks had been replaced by *fusslappen*, small pieces of cloth, now wrapped around the feet and secured by a pair of old boot-laces.

Most of the postcards home were without sentiment and very much to the point, and read something like the following:

45

'Am safe but a prisoner-of-war. Am not wounded and quite well. Please send me, as soon as possible, a large parcel containing cigarettes, chocolate, condensed milk, sweets, tins of meat, tins of fruit, and some dog biscuits.'

The requests for the dog biscuits were included on the advice of an amateur dietitian in the camp.

During the following two weeks, the bed bugs, fleas, and lice arrived, more or less in that order. As we felt that we could not be held responsible for the arrival of the bed bugs and fleas, they were accepted philosophically as just one more thing we had to bear. It was the lice that made us feel degraded. Shamed by the thought that they had probably been bred in our own filth, most of us sought a surreptitious and losing battle with them beneath the privacy of our blankets. Later we became less sensitive, and all delousing was done in the latrines, where there were always a row of squatting, silent men, absorbed in the task of plucking lice from the seams of their clothing.

The hot summer days passed slowly, dead days of despair, spent following out a routine that never changed. At six o'clock every morning there was a check parade that went on for ages, while the guards trotted up and down, laboriously miscounting us at least a dozen times before reaching the correct answer. After the guards had stamped off, there were some half-hearted ablutions carried out without the benefit of soap, and then a general retirement back to bed to await the arrival of the midday soup. In the afternoon, however, the camp took on a sudden appearance of life. Men taking their daily constitutional, shuffled slowly and painfully along the paths in their clogs, or clattered through the different barracks in endless streams, hoping to pick some latrine rumour that would send them back to their own barrack buoyed with false optimism. After the bread ration had been issued, the camp became quiet again while we leaned against the barrack walls or sat in the dust watching the sun go down. Just before dark the guards came into the camp and counted us again. After that we went inside to face the night.

It was during an afternoon stroll around the barracks that I came across a man who owned a book, probably the only book in Stalag VIIIB at that time. He was sitting on a top bunk reading with beetle-browed concentration, his feet dangling in space, and seeing that he was already on the last few pages, I moved forward hopefully.

'What's the book, chum?' I said loudly, plucking at his trouser leg.

The man silently held the book out for me to see the title, and then continued with his reading.

I waited until he had read another page. 'I see you've nearly finished it,' I said.

Silence.

I coughed. 'I suppose you wouldn't like to lend it to me.'

This time the man spoke. 'You've got a hope!' Closing the book, he placed it on the bed beside him. 'I'll sell it to you, though.'

'How much?' I asked wearily.

'One day's bread ration,' the man said.

'I'll think about it,' I said.

Slowly I walked back to my own barrack. Much as I wanted the book, I was not keen on giving up a day's ration of bread for it. On the other hand, if I could persuade Charlie and Albert to come in on the deal, I was quite prepared to give up a third of my ration. The trouble was that neither Charlie nor Albert struck me as being reading men. It was not going to be easy.

I found the two of them sitting on the barrack steps, gloomily watching the stream of men going in and out of the latrines. Sitting down beside them, I said: 'I've just met a man who's got a book.'

Charlie grunted. 'He must have wanted something to do, lugging a book around with him all through the march.'

It was not a very encouraging start.

'As a matter of fact,' I said casually, 'I thought it might be a good idea if we bought it from him. He's willing to sell.'

'I bet he is,' Albert said. 'What's he want for it?'

'Bread,' I said.

'Bread for a book!' Charlie said, his voice rising. 'Don't be bloody stupid!'

'If we bought it, we would be the only people around here with a book,' I said quickly. 'When things improve, we'll be able to lend it out for bread, cigarettes—all sorts of things. Try and think of it as a long-term policy—an investment for the future.'

'What future?' Charlie said. 'The way things are going, we won't be around that long.'

'What's the name of the book?' Albert asked idly.

'*Miss Brown of X.Y.O.* . . . It's a thriller by Phillips Oppenheim,' I added quickly, hoping that it would help.

'I don't care what it is,' Charlie said, 'I'm not giving bread for a book, and that's final.' He grinned. 'But if you're set on having it, I'm quite willing to have a go at pinching it.'

'You know, Charlie,' I said slowly, 'I think that's rather a good idea. The bloke who's got this book really deserves to have it pinched. He's read the book, and instead of passing it on to one of his comrades, which would be no skin off his nose, he tries to flog it.'

'Sounds a proper bastard,' Charlie said solemnly. 'Now let's have your ideas how we set about the job.'

Unfortunately, when we got down to it neither Albert nor I were able to produce a plan good enough to satisfy Charlie.

'A lot of help you are,' Charlie said in disgust, after the last scheme had been put forward and rejected. 'I can see I'll have to do the job myself. It'll probably be safer, anyway. Just show me where the bloke hangs out, and then leave me to get on with it."

So I took Charlie along to the barracks, discreetly pointed out the man with the book, and then returned to the barrack to wait with Albert for Charlie's return. In less than ten minutes, Charlie was with us again.

'Easy as kiss my arse,' Charlie said, throwing the book on my bed. 'It was just a matter of waiting for the right moment.'

I looked at him in admiration. 'I don't know how you do it, Charlie.'

'Natural talent, I suppose,' Charlie said modestly.

Miss Brown of X.Y.O. proved to be most enjoyable. It was read by nearly a hundred prisoners before it finally disintegrated and came to an ignominious but useful end as toilet-paper.

Thieving had started up during the first week at Stalag, and now hardly a day passed without someone having his bread ration stolen from under his very nose by some nimble-fingered prisoner. The result was that we trusted nobody. It was therefore unfortunate that the Sergeant-Majors should decide to supervise the ladling out of the midday soup. Sergeant-Majors, possibly through no fault of their own, are never very popular with the ranks, and as we were already suspicious of each other, it was not surprising that we should be only too willing to suspect a Sergeant-Major of trying to cheat us.

In our suspicious minds, it seemed to us that the ladling out of the soup was conducted under extremely fishy circumstances. Every lunch hour one of the barracks was emptied, and into it stalked a Sergeant-Major, followed by several minions carrying the soup buckets. The barrack door was closed with a decisive bang, and then, after what seemed to us a rather long lapse, a window opened to reveal the Sergeant-Major brandishing a ladle. After we had all been up to the window to receive a ladleful of soup, carefully levelled off before it was slopped into our dixies, the window closed, and a few seconds later the Sergeant-Major and his minions appeared again with the now empty buckets.

We're being done all right, we thought darkly as we

watched them go. What do you think they're doing in there before they open that window? Swigging the soup, of course. Why do you think they're so careful how they dole it out? So that there's still some over for them afterwards. Here's us with hardly enough soup to fill a squirt pistol, and there they are, pouring it down them by the gallon every day. And so on, and so on.

There was possibly no foundation at all to our suspicions, but imagined or otherwise it did not help the general morale of the camp. Relations between the ranks and the N.C.O.s deteriorated still further, when they decided that the time had come to show the Germans that the British prisoners were not so demoralized as they looked. With blithe unconcern for the fact that the rations were only just about enough to keep us on our feet, they announced that from now on there would be P.T. exercises every morning.

The next morning we reluctantly crawled out to show the Germans that we were not demoralized, and while a Sergeant-Major stood firmly rooted to one spot, bawling away happily, we half-heartedly went through a series of exercises. In the background a German Unteroffizier and a number of guards watched and nodded approvingly. After it was all over, the Unteroffizier made a little speech on the importance of keeping fit, and ended with the promise that if we kept it up we would receive a piece of cake every afternoon.

The promised cake never turned up, and after a while the P.T. parades became such a farce that they were finally dropped. Afterwards we convinced ourselves that the cake idea had been something cooked up between our own N.C.O.s and the Germans to keep us attending the P.T. parades for as long as possible. We were always ready to believe the worst of anyone.

In the situation that we were in, we should have at least been united in our common plight. But we were not united. Hunger, black despair, and the bitter lessons we had learnt on the march had changed us. Fear of the future and a mistrust of everyone poisoned all our thinking, and often led to violent quarrels; quarrels, for instance, like the one between myself and Charlie and Albert.

It was the bread ration that brought us to the final parting of the ways. Ever since we had been at the camp, we had daily gone through the bread-cutting ritual with no more trouble beyond the general mild bickering that went on everywhere during the bread-slicing period. Just before the bread was due to arrive on the afternoon of the quarrel, the routine was unfortunately broken. I went over to the latrines and spent rather a long time there on a delousing session. When I returned, I found Albert and Charlie on their bunks. Charlie was holding a portion of bread in his hand, studying it idly.

'You're late,' Charlie said. 'The bread ration came up ages ago. Albert said he was hungry and couldn't wait, so I've already cut the bread. You'll find yours on the bed.'

'I've been keeping an eye on it,' Albert said, his mouth full with the last remains of his bread.

I was feeling depressed and irritable. I had found even more lice than usual that day, and, discouraged by the losing battle I was fighting with them, had come back looking for trouble. Going over to my bed, I picked up the piece of bread and looked at it morosely. It seemed distinctly smaller than usual. Then I looked at the piece of bread in Charlie's hand.

'That looks like a big third you've got there,' I said.

'It's exactly the same as yours,' Charlie said coldly.

'In that case, you won't mind changing with me,' I said.

There was a long silence. Then Charlie slowly lifted his head from the pillow. Staring down at me, he said quietly: 'Are you saying I've twisted you over the bread?'

'That's right,' I said, 'I am.'

Charlie looked at Albert, who started to whistle tunelessly.

'Did I ever twist you on the march?' Charlie said finally.

'I never gave you the chance,' I said.

'Well, I'm . . .' Charlie said. He took a deep breath. 'Listen. If I give you this piece of bread in my hand in exchange for the piece you've got, I'd be admitting that I twisted you. So,' Charlie said, 'I'm not going to do it.'

'All right,' I said, 'keep it. But from now on, I'm on my own.'

'You certainly are,' Charlie said. 'And I hope you rot.'

And after that the two of them never spoke to me again.

Ours was just one of the petty quarrels that led to a break-up in partnerships that had weathered a great deal up to this point. In our case I was entirely to blame. As a result of it, I found myself walking around the camp alone and without friends, and sharing my bread ration with two strangers who really did need watching.

Stalag VIIIB was the main camp for prisoners throughout the whole war, and as such reflected the general morale of the British prisoner. The spirit of the prisoners in it in 1940 was admittedly very poor, but there was some reason for its being so. In later years most of the world was united against Nazism. Troops of all nations fought side by side for a common cause in which the issues seemed very clear, and although there were continual defeats, there was always the knowledge that troops were carrying on the battle somewhere else. In 1940 it was a little different. A year after the abortive Munich agreement we had suddenly found ourselves in uniform, being trained to take our part in a war which had been embarked upon without any particular enthusiasm. After the first few anxious weeks, the war proved to be a 'phoney war', and we were lulled into a false sense of security by the lack of news and military training that reflected no sense of urgency. But suddenly the war had turned out to be something very real, and within the space of a few weeks we found ourselves prisoners, our allies defeated and occupied, and England herself on the brink of defeat. We had come in at the tail end of an era of non-realistic thinking, and we were crushed and bewildered by the price that had had to be paid for it. The sour smell of defeat was in our nostrils, and there seemed no hope of ever getting rid of it again. Looking for the scapegoats, we blamed the French and the Belgians for letting the Germans through; we blamed our own generals who had sent us into the field half-trained and ill-equipped to fight against an enemy that had everything, and we blamed the newspapers for encouraging apathy and false confidence with stories like the one of the Germans using wooden tanks in Poland. It was therefore not surprising that our morale was not all that it should have been.

To make matters worse, at that stage we did not even hate the Germans. Before the war we had grown up in an age in which the evils of Nazism had been played down, and despite some knowledge of the persecution of the Jews and of the concentration camps, the Germans were still just 'Jerry' to us, and not members of a nation capable of mass extermination.

Fortunately, after a period of readjustment our attitude changed, and we settled down to make the best of things. How well we succeeded in doing this could be seen in much of the daily life of Stalag VIIIB in later years. Although my visits to the camp were limited to occasional trips to collect books for my working party, I saw enough to make the memory of all that happened there in 1940 seem rather like an unpleasant dream.

The British compound later became highly organized, and made for itself a way of life which simulated, as much as it was possible, civilian life and most of its social amenities. The only thing that the camp lacked in the way of entertainment was a cinema. It had everything else. There was a symphony orchestra, a dance band, and a theatre that put on modern plays, Shakespeare, revues and musicals, including *Oklahoma*, which was put on in Stalag VIIIB several years before the show arrived in London. Although the camp was hardly in a position to boast of having a public-house, a number of public-spirited individuals did their best to fill this gap with Schnapps made in home-made stills and brewed with the help of potato-peelings, rotting vegetables, and raisins from the Red Cross parcels. For the more studious, there were lectures, classes on a large variety of subjects, and correspondence courses to help pass the years of imprisonment.

Despite the restrictions that were imposed on the individual, the camp still managed to create various stratas of society. There were the rich, ranging from Gordon Rolls, the millionaire, who had a self-appointed batman of his own, to prisoners who lived in comparative luxury, buying more or less what they wanted with the many cigarette parcels they received from home. There were also the poor, who received no cigarette parcels, and had to rely on the Red Cross to supplement German rations that were only a little better than those received in 1940. There were 'wide' boys who roamed the camp selling packets of tea, half filled with sawdust, or tins of condensed milk from which the milk had been siphoned out and replaced with water before being resealed. There were petty crooks, big-time racketeers, and men who had been used to backing up an argument with a razor. Among all these moved the other prisoners—the average prisoner—who went about his business, making the best of things and waiting patiently for the end.

The racketeers supplied much of the lighter side of Stalag VIIIB, and their swap-shops were one of the unique features of the camp. Every day sections of the camp resembled Petticoat Lane, with the stall-holders busily exhorting the passing crowd to buy or sell. The stalls, which were forms borrowed from the barracks, were often covered with a blanket, owing to the illegal nature of the things for sale or exchange. Beneath the blankets were German bayonets, watches, vicious-looking knives, concertinas, cut-throat razors, and even wireless-sets guaranteed to work. As the wireless-sets had been smuggled into the camp at some considerable risk, the price tag on them was very high—500 cigarettes.

The camp had its grimmer aspects, and one of them was the Germans' inhuman treatment of the Russian prisoners, who died there literally in thousands. On their arrival at the camp, in the depths of an almost Siberian winter, they had been forced to spend the days and nights in an open field, until hundreds of them died from exposure. When a typhus epidemic swept through Stalag VIIIB, they were again left to die without medical attention, and every morning a cart would tour their camp, collecting the dead and the dying, who were all thrown into a mass grave, the still-living with the dead. Although conditions improved for them a little afterwards, the gaunt skeletons in rags who came into the British compounds to clean out the latrines were a constant reminder of what the Germans were capable of doing to a race whom they considered were *Untermenschen*.

But, on the whole, little disturbed the tenor of the life the prisoners had made for themselves. The years passed slowly and nothing changed much, despite the occasional visits by Swiss Red Cross representatives, whose suggestions for improvements were carefully noted by the Germans, and then promptly forgotten as soon as the representatives were outside the gate. Despite the disciplined air of the camp, there was always something going on that would have given the Kommandant an apoplectic fit if he had known about it. There were the wireless-sets that were tuned in every night for the news from London; there was the bribing of the search guards, who could be persuaded with a packet of cigarettes not to examine too closely the effects of a prisoner returning from a working party, and worst of all, as far as the Germans were concerned, there was the occasional swapping over of identities between the R.A.F. and soldiers. Any airman planning an escape knew that his best bet was to get on to one of the working parties, where there were generally plenty of opportunities of making an easy getaway. As R.A.F. personnel were not allowed out of the camp, the potential escapee solved the problem by finding some soldier who was due to be sent out to work and who wished for nothing more than the opportunity of spending the rest of his prisoner days in camp. Uniforms were changed and discs swapped, and the airman went off to try his luck, leaving the soldier to enjoy his new-found leisure.

Life in Stalag VIIIB was not without its dramatic moments. Sometimes a prisoner was shot or someone hanged himself miserably in the latrines; and on one occasion there was a murder—an unsolved murder. The body was found in a pond of static water that was kept in the camp for use in case of fire. The pond was shallow, certainly not deep enough for anyone to fall into and drown himself, and the body that was fished out of it posed several questions that were never answered. It had obviously been there for some time, for its face was a blurred mass of sodden and decaying flesh, no longer identifiable. The body itself was dressed in a German uniform, but the strange thing was that, officially at least, the Germans had not missed one of their guards. It was also a little odd how the body had got there in the first place. The body could not have been placed in the pond in broad daylight, with prisoners passing by all the time, and in the evening the guards were not in the habit of going through the camp. There were countless rumours, but it remained an unsolved mystery.

Stalag VIIIB ended its life as a prisoner-of-war camp when the Russians swept into Germany, when it was immediately evacuated and all its prisoners taken out on the road to join the other columns of prisoners being driven towards the Germans' intended last stronghold in Southern Germany. But that was in 1945. In the summer of 1940 we had not the slightest idea that the war was going to last that long, or that it would spread across most of the globe before it finally ended. All we knew then was that the war already seemed nearly finished and that we were on the losing side of it. Meanwhile, the days dragged on, and we became weaker and weaker, until in the end it was an effort to even walk around the camp. Personally worried over the fact that I was now passing water the colour of brown ale, I was beginning to wonder whether we would ever see the end, imminent as it seemed.

Our salvation came with an announcement from the Germans that volunteers were wanted for a large number of working parties that were due to leave the camp within the next few days. Although there was something vaguely reminiscent of British Army tactics in the way they also stated that work was compulsory anyway, we needed no urging to volunteer. The food on working parties, we had been assured, would be far better than the camp rations, for prisoners would be fed by the civilians for whom they were working. With rather misguided ideas on the generosity of factory owners, mine owners, lumber-camp bosses, and other German civilians responsible for our future welfare, we rushed to get our names on the working lists. As all the jobs offered seemed equally unpleasant, I put my name down for the first job that came along—that of a labourer at a cement factory outside Oppeln, a town near the Polish border.

On the surface of it, we now had some cause to be a little more optimistic about our future. There was now the prospect of more food and better conditions, a change of scenery, and, among a small group of men on a working party, the chance of some consideration as an individual, instead of being an anonymous figure lost in the homogeneous mass of men that milled around the camp—or so we thought. We still had a great deal to learn about the Germans.

CHAPTER FOUR

Working Party

THE thirty men who lined up to depart for the cement factory were an ill-assorted lot—a few battered Regulars who had sweated out most of their time in the East; a number of North Countrymen who had been industrial workers in civvy street; a few call-ups, whose horizons before that had never extended much beyond local 'hops' and the Odeon; a stately, middle-aged man who had been a Cook's courier, an architect, a commercial artist, a bank clerk, a carpet layer, a farm-hand, and a number of others who had caught a daily bus, tube, or train to an office desk somewhere in the City or the West End of London.

Later this party was to split up into three factions—the Regulars, living in a private world of past adventures in foreign brothels and booze-ups from Aldershot to Cairo; the industrial workers, aggressive and contemptuous of the fumbling, weak-backed white-collar workers, and the white-collar workers, who tried, unsuccessfully, not to show their dismay at having to rub their lower-middle-class refinement against the rougher elements of the party. Thirty men who would have got on tolerably well in normal army life were to find it quite impossible to do so shut up in the close confines of a small room, with never a moment's escape from each other.

But on that summer's morning, waiting to set off to catch the train, we were friendly and talkative, united in the happy thought that we were leaving Stalag VIIIB with the prospect of more food, better living conditions, and a chance to live.

A few minutes after we had lined up, a Feldwebel and two guards came along and took over from the British Sergeant. The Feldwebel was a chubby little man, red faced and amiable. The guards were less prepossessing—one a cadaverous-looking individual with a face like a death's head, the other a stout man of about forty-five who looked like a disgruntled butcher and scowled all the time. Two opposites who looked as if they had been paired off as natural music-hall foils. We were to find out that there was nothing funny about these guards, except their appearance when they were together. The boot, the gun butt, the voice used at top pitch, those were to be the familiar associations with these two. And yet the Feldwebel, the happy, smiling Feldwebel who stood there beaming at us, was to be the worst of the three. The Feldwebel, it turned out later, was a 'case'. In the years to come, when more and more men were needed for the front, and anything male and still standing on two legs was used to guard prisoners, we were to get quite used to people like the Feldwebel. The Feldwebel barked out an order, grinned, and then pranced skittishly towards the gate. The two guards watched him sourly and indicated for us to follow.

It also seemed a promising sign for the future when we reached the railway siding and found third-class carriages awaiting us instead of the usual cattle trucks. Clambering into one of the compartments, I immediately investigated the ash-trays. They were full to the brim. There was a hasty division of the butts, and then we were relaxing contentedly against the wooden walls of the compartment, puffing away at our squashed and soggy ends, while the train moved out of the siding and then made its way slowly across the flat and uninteresting Upper Silesian countryside.

Our good humour vanished as soon as we reached Oppeln. Stepping out of the station into the bright sunlight, we were immediately greeted by a delighted howl from a group of small boys, who joyfully attached themselves to our rear. Scowling and muttering among ourselves, we shuffled out of the station yard into the main road, where great droves of grinning townsfolk promptly began to gather on the pavements to watch us pass. Ignoring them, we struggled on, trying not to lose our clogs that threatened to part company with us at every step. The clogs had seemed bad enough in Stalag VIIIB, where we had moved about more or less in our own time. Hurrying along that main road and dodging traffic that seemed deliberately bent on edging us into the gutter, they were a monstrous hindrance to progress.

While we had been in Stalag VIIIB, we had not been particularly conscious of anything ridiculous in our appearance as we had shuffled around in our clogs and tattered remnants of French, Belgian, and Polish uniforms. The people of Oppeln seemed anxious to bring to our attention just how ridiculous we did look. Every so often some wag in the crowd would shout out something which we did not understand, and immediately all the women around him would go into peals of laughter. The sight of those healthy and mostly good-looking females tittering away at us was the most devastating thing that had happened to us since we had been captured. It was the knock-out blow to whatever pride we might have had left.

Finally, we were out of the town and walking along a quiet country road. We shambled along it for about an hour, and then ahead of us loomed the cement factory, a great, rambling building, covered with a fine coating of cement dust. A few minutes later we came to a halt in front of a stone building, inside the yard of the factory. In front of the building was a small compound about twenty feet square and surrounded by barbed wire. This, the Feldwebel told us, was our new *Lager*. We were not impressed.

There was no window to the building, only a fanlight above the stout iron doors, that were open, revealing a dark, uninviting interior. We filed dismally through the compound into the building, where the Feldwebel switched on the light to reveal our living quarters. In front of us was a long, narrow room with fifteen double-tiered bunks and a small open space for two long tables and forms. But it was the tables that were the first thing we really noticed. Thirty places had been laid out on them for a meal; thirty new, shining bowls, and beside each bowl a knife, fork, and spoon. Above the tables, on one of the walls, was a shelf with thirty mugs hanging on hooks in a neat row. Even as we stood there staring, two German civilians came in behind us carrying a huge bucket of carrot soup. The Feldwebel and the two guards were almost knocked down in the frenzied rush as we made for the tables.

The two civilians had only just finished ladling out the soup when another civilian arrived on the scene; a short, dapper little man with a spiked moustache and beady eyes. He watched us in silence until we had finished our meal, and then called for the interpreter. Percy, the ex-Cook's courier, sailed majestically forward to do the honours.

'I am sorry the food was not better,' the little man said, 'but we had to get it prepared in a hurry so that it would be ready for you when you arrived. Tomorrow it will be better —much better. Meanwhile, I will see that some bread is brought in to you.'

Almost as one man we stood up and cheered.

'I can see you are all good fellows and will work hard,' the little man said, beaming at us. Taking their cue from him, the Feldwebel and the two guards also smiled, a little mechanically I thought. 'You start work tomorrow,' the little man said, still smiling. 'You all look strong fellows. You should not find the work too hard. Anyway, you will certainly find it varied and interesting.'

Everyone in the room had taken a liking to the little man. In fact, all the Germans in the room at that moment seemed jolly good fellows; the two civilians holding the soup bucket, the red-faced Feldwebel, the guard with a face like a death's head; even the other guard, who wasn't smiling, was obviously a jolly good fellow, although he wasn't showing it right at that moment. At long last our real troubles were over. The references to hard work had been a little ominous, but we were sure that everything would turn out all right.

The little man seemed very friendly and sympathetic, and would no doubt make allowances if we were not quite up to scratch in the beginning.

The guards and the civilians departed, and we were left alone for an hour to talk excitedly among ourselves of our good fortune. Then the doors opened again and the guards came in carrying a huge latrine bucket. This was for use during the night, and had to be emptied daily. We were a little dampened by this rather unsanitary arrangement, until someone noticed a loudspeaker above the door. A wireless, as well. What more could we want? A few minutes later the lights went out. The promised bread had not arrived, but it did not really matter. We would be getting more food tomorrow—the little man had said so.

At about four-thirty the next morning we were awakened by the shattering roar of martial music coming from the loudspeaker above the door. The sound of it was enough to awaken the dead. As we slowly emerged from beneath the blankets and gazed blearily around us, the steel doors clanged open and the stout guard stamped in, bellowing at the top of his voice.

The man in the top bunk nearest the door sat up, looked down with horror at the guard, and then dived beneath the blankets again. The guard promptly caught him by the legs and pulled. Frantically anchoring himself to the bedpost, the prisoner cried hoarsely for help, and then, losing his grip on the post, fell to the floor amid a jumble of blankets.

It was at that moment that the Feldwebel arrived on the scene, carrying a long bamboo stick and dressed only in his shirt and trousers. As he stood there in the doorway with his braces trailing on the ground behind him, I thought for a moment that he had come to remonstrate with the guard for his unnecessary cruelty. I was wrong. Suddenly the Feldwebel gave an unearthly scream, and with the agility of a ballet-dancer executing a *grande jete*, he leapt up on to the table nearest the door. The next moment he was running along the table, using his bamboo stick to sweep our soup bowls off the shelf that ran along the wall above the table. Reaching the other end of the table, he leapt off, and then ran shouting out of the room. I looked at the soup bowls now scattered all over the floor, and then at the guard who was still bawling and pulling prisoners from their bunks. From the moment of the Feldwebel's arrival to his departure he had not taken the slightest notice of him. He was evidently a little more used to the Feldwebel than we were.

About a quarter of an hour later we were all dressed and ready for work. Just before we went outside in the chill early morning air for our first day's work for the German Reich, the two guards brought in a can of ersatz coffee to share among ourselves. This was breakfast.

The little man must have had a peculiar idea of what was varied and interesting work, for the work consisted mostly of non-stop shovelling with a spade almost as big as oneself. There was coal to unload from wagons, gypsum to load into wagons, sand to shovel down ravenously hungry hoppers, and furnaces to feed with coal-dust that was eaten up by the fires almost before it had left the shovel.

As a change one could work in the packing department and carry sacks of cement all day, or alternatively, work in the nearby quarry under a demon foreman who raved and screamed from the moment you arrived until knocking-off time.

We worked twelve hours a day, with an hour's break for lunch, when we sat down to a bowl of soup. At six o'clock in the evening we returned to another bowl of soup, three boiled potatoes, and three slices of bread, which we were supposed to save for breakfast. Sunday was a day of rest, with nothing to do but lie on one's bunk and think of home and wait for the midday meal, when we also received a small rissole as well as the usual bowl of soup.

Each week we received four marks ninety pfennigs, in *Lager geld* for the week's work. This camp money, specially issued for prisoners-of-war, was almost useless, as the only things we could buy with it were razor-blades, ersatz soup powders, and occasionally, if we were very lucky, tobacco leaf which we chopped up and rolled into practically unsmokable cigarettes.

The little man who had greeted us on our arrival turned out to be the factory chemist and general stooge for the directors. We were no longer on speaking terms. He was, we found out, just one more German who handed out promises with no intention of keeping them. He was equally disappointed with us. For some strange reason, the English did not share the German factory workers' enthusiasm for work. In fact, they seemed inclined to dodge it at every possible opportunity. I think he was really quite hurt at the thought.

Most weekdays I came back to the billet, had a very perfunctory wash in the workmen's washrooms, and then fell into bed and went to sleep immediately. Generally, I didn't stir until the next morning, when the blaring wireless brought me staggering out of bed like a punch-drunk boxer answering the bell. Sundays were a little better. On Sunday there was time for soulful and rather self-pitying meditation on the bed, a leisurely shower after lunch, and then a period for quiet conversation with friends.

It was on one of these afternoons that I settled down at a table with Steve and Tommy for a serious discussion on food, a subject on all our minds, all day and every day. Both Tommy and Steve were from my own regiment; Tommy was a tall, lugubrious-looking man with a permanently sad expression, rather like that of an abandoned bloodhound; Steve a thick-set and burly man with a face like a prizefighter, and not a man you would think given to an æsthetic appreciation of food. But on that afternoon Steve sounded like a gourmet, dwelling with wistful appreciation on past meals that had been specially prepared for him by some of the best chefs in Europe.

'There was a café where I used to go,' Steve said, 'where the food was delicious.' The way Steve rolled the word 'delicious' around his tongue was really rather pathetic. He then began to describe in great detail the sort of menu that the café provided. It didn't sound as if it had been a very good café.

'Talking of menus,' Tommy said suddenly, 'I've prepared one myself. It covers four meals a day for a week—breakfast, lunch, dinner, and supper.'

We looked at him in silence, wondering if perhaps life was getting a little too much for him.

'This menu,' Tommy said a little self-consciously, 'is what I'm going to have to eat the first week I get back home.' He fumbled in his pocket and pulled out a dog-eared piece of paper. Steve and I looked at the menu. It was certainly an interesting one. In making up four meals a day for a week, Tommy had managed to work in enough food to keep a regiment going for some considerable time.

'And you're going to eat all this in a week,' I said.

'I think I can manage it,' Tommy said modestly.

This preoccupation with the subject of food sometimes took a strange turn, far more frightening than Tommy's harmless menu. There was one prisoner, for instance, who had managed to get hold of a packet of coloured crayons, and with these drew crude, surrealistic pictures of food, which he would hang on the wall above his bed and stare at for hours. Others hoarded what little bread they received, keeping it under their pillows until it was stale and almost uneatable. Some of the prisoners considered the hoarders fair prey, and stole their bread at the first opportunity. If caught, as they sometimes were, they tried to justify themselves by pointing out that if someone kept bread, they didn't really need it, anyway. In that, at least, most of us were in agreement with them.

Already the camp was split by our inability to live together. The work itself did not help matters either. All the white-collar workers were quite hopeless with a shovel, and put in a truck with other men were quite likely to brain someone, or deposit the contents of the shovel in their neighbour's face instead of out of the truck. Those who had been used to manual labour were quite naturally more than a little impatient with us, especially as they had to do more work on account of our inefficiency. They were not slow to tell us exactly what they thought of us. Acutely conscious of our own inadequacy, we immediately retaliated by saying that we had no intention of working more than was absolutely necessary, and if they cared to slave their guts out for the Germans, they were quite at liberty to do so. But, of course, if they did they realized they were little better than traitors. This state of affairs continued for some time, with both sides loathing the other, and it was not until people like myself were able to perform with a shovel with a reasonable degree of efficiency that an uneasy truce was made.

The winter began to draw near, and the canker of despair ate even deeper into us. There was nothing to bolster us up; no letters from home, no good news; not even the comradeship of sharing a common adversity. The food got worse, the Feldwebel got madder and madder, and the guards more unpleasant and brutal with every passing day. And, of course, there were the lice, bigger and fatter than ever and breeding like fury. They drove us to distraction during the day and kept us occupied for hours every night while we sat on our bunks hunting them down, cracking them between our nails, and afterwards running matches down the seams of our clothes to burn the eggs. None of this, I might add, had the slightest effect.

Now that we were a little more used to the work and not quite so tired in the evenings, time dragged more slowly than ever. The only reading material we could get hold of was an occasional German newspaper, full of reports of London in flames, generally accompanied by a depressing night picture taken over London during a raid. Eventually, however, a German newspaper for prisoners called *The Camp* arrived. This was a four-page effort, with a leader article, loaded with subtle propaganda, a series of inoffensive snippets from English newspapers, and some general articles on the progress of the war. Gradually, as the years went by, the paper became more and more inoffensive, until in the end it consisted mostly of short stories and articles written by the prisoners themselves.

I decided to brush up my German to help while away the time, and after I had made an application to Stalag VIIIB for some text-books, two very good grammar-books arrived. From then on I spent an hour or so every evening studying German with Arthur, another Queen Vic, who also had the same idea as I had in the back of my mind—to become proficient enough at the language to take over the job of a camp interpreter if the opportunity ever arose.

Finally the winter arrived, bringing with it bleak winds from Russia that chilled us to the bone as we stood shivering outside the factory unloading the coal wagons that came into the yard in an endless stream. Clothing was now a serious problem. A supply of Belgian overcoats had been sent out to us from Stalag VIIIB, but as these were all torn and threadbare, they afforded little protection against the bitter cold. Our shirts were now nothing more than rags, our *fusslappen* either lost or in shreds. Seeking a way to increase our wardrobe, we stole paper cement bags from the packing department and made shirts from them. Newspapers scrounged from the workers made a satisfactory substitute for the *fusslappen*.

Up to this point we had worked as best we could so as to keep ourselves out of trouble. Now, with the working conditions as bad as they were and the rations so small as to be practically non-existent, it began to occur to us that we really had very little to lose whatever happened. Suddenly, all our internal strife and petty bickering were forgotten in a united decision to do as little work as possible and to cause as much trouble as we could.

Until then the guards had had a pretty easy time of it. Each morning they had both taken us to work, had a friendly chat with the foreman, and then retired to their room to read or sleep, emerging only occasionally for a leisurely and rather bored tour of the factory. We changed all that within a matter of days. Suddenly the guards found themselves involved almost hourly in a game of hide-and-seek with some prisoner or other who had left his job for a quiet stroll around the factory. Whenever a prisoner was caught he always had an answer—an order had been mis-understood; he was looking for a better shovel or for the foreman to discuss a problem that had arisen about the un-loading of some wagons. The guard would then proceed to boot the prisoner back to his job, the prisoner philosophic-ally accepting the kicks, happily conscious that he had done nothing for at least a couple of hours.

Two Geordies outdid the lot of us. Finding a plank of wood in the factory, they carried it backwards and forwards from the quarry to the factory for several days before they were finally caught out. The fact that they had expended a great deal of energy in walking was of no importance. The important thing was that no constructive work had been done for the factory during that time.

One of our happier moments came soon afterwards, when Tommy and I were sent to work in the packing department. We had been working for some time, filling the wagons with bags of cement, when Tommy suddenly called me over to one of the wagons.

'This truck is already loaded,' he said.

'Good,' I said. 'That's one less for us to do.'

'It's loaded with bags of ersatz coffee,' Tommy said, 'not bags of cement. They must have tacked this wagon on by mistake at the marshalling yard.' He looked at the sacks. 'Pity we can't find some way of sabotaging this lot.'

'You sabotage them,' I said. 'But not while I'm around. I'm not that tired of life.'

'You know what,' Tommy said thoughtfully, 'we could pee on them. That would be safe enough.'

I looked at the stacked-up sacks of coffee. 'I rather like that idea,' I said slowly. 'But you and I are not really capable of doing a thorough job of it.'

'We need assistance,' Tommy said. 'I don't think this is a

thing we should keep to ourselves, anyway. I'll pass the word around.'

Tommy disappeared, and soon after that prisoners came in a steady stream, from all parts of the factory, to baptize the sacks, while Tommy and I kept an eye out for the foreman.

Until then the one place I had managed to avoid working in was the quarry. This had been accomplished only by being more hopeless, more lazy, and more inefficient than anyone else; more a matter of natural temperament rather than any praiseworthy attempts on my part to avoid working for the Germans. But at last my turn came for a brief but spectacular career as a quarry worker.

I was working away quite happily in the factory, sweeping away some of the everlasting piles of dust that gathered in every corner of it, when the guard came for me.

'I'm taking you down to the quarry,' he said. 'They're a man short down there today.'

'I don't want to work in the quarry,' I said. I turned and pointed to another prisoner working nearby. 'Look. There's a man who likes working in the open air. Why don't you take him?'

But the guard had obviously made up his mind, and a few minutes later I was trailing miserably behind him as we made our way towards the quarry.

Czok, the foreman, was waiting at the entrance of the quarry for us. A stout little man with pig-like eyes and a voice like a eunuch.

'A new one,' Czok said, looking me up and down. I had the feeling that he was not very impressed. Indicating for me to follow him, Czok led the way across the quarry until we came to a cut in the ground. The cut was about twenty feet wide and about four feet deep, with a sloping path carrying a set of rails for bucket wagons to be pushed in and out of it. The bottom of the cut was hidden from sight, covered with about four inches of water. There was also a wagon there, and leaning against it a pick and shovel.

Czok pointed towards the wagon. 'It's not hard work. All you have to do is to pick stone from the side, load the wagon, push it out, and take it over to the other end of the quarry, where you unload it and get another wagon. When you've filled twenty wagons, you can go back to your *Lager*.'

I looked at the wagon, at the pick, and finally at the water at the bottom of the cut. Then I looked at Czok. The expression on his face told me there was no point in arguing. Soon I was up to my knees in water, feebly picking at the sides of the cut. After I had been at it for about a quarter of an hour, I had still succeeded in making only a few minute indentations in the rock. Czok stood behind me, watching. He seemed fascinated. I continued to swing away until I had finally managed to hack out a piece of stone about the size of a large cricket ball. Behind me Czok cheered ironically. I began picking away again, a little harder this time as I heard Czok splashing through the water towards me. Suddenly, rather to my surprise, another small piece of rock came away and fell quietly into the water at my feet.

'*Lieber Gott*,' Czok said behind me. 'Is that the best you can do?'

'On a bowl of potato soup—yes,' I said.

Czok stared at me, and it suddenly occurred to me that he was embarrassed. Growling under his breath, he snatched the pick from my hands and threw it into the wagon. Beckoning me to follow him, he led the way across the quarry until we finally came to a halt in front of a fair-sized locomotive. Czok screamed something, and a man clambered out of the engine and lumbered slowly towards us.

'Conrad,' Czok said, 'I've brought you an Englishman to help you. He's no good, but you might find some use for him.'

I looked at Conrad. He was at least six feet two, built like a giant, and with a face that looked as if it had been carved out of granite. He was also obviously very drunk. Czok was either blind and oblivious to the smell of Schnapps that hung in the air around us, or he was used to Conrad being drunk. Anyway, he said nothing, and after a few casual remarks about the weather he left us.

As soon as he had gone, the huge German turned to me. 'You work well for me and I'll see you get food,' Conrad said thickly. 'If you don't work . . .' Leaving the sentence unfinished, he spat on the ground.

The job was simple enough. As Conrad drove the train around the quarry, picking up the various loaded trucks ready to be taken to the huge crusher, it was my task to ride on the footplate, ready to jump off and run ahead to switch over the points whenever necessary. Everything went well for a while. It was warm inside the engine, and after Conrad had taken numerous swigs from the Schnapps bottle he was carrying in his pocket, he became quite friendly. We had almost done a complete circuit of the quarry and were nearing the engine shed, when Conrad saw that he had forgotten to pick up some trucks on the other side of the quarry.

'Switch the points over to the right,' Conrad bawled. 'Get moving.'

Jumping off the footplate, I ran forward to the points and switched them over. It was not until the train had gone past me, heading for the engine shed, that I realized I had switched the points over the wrong way.

Inside the cabin, Conrad was happily bawling a popular song, beating time with the Schnapps bottle, quite unaware that he was heading in the wrong direction. The next moment there was a splintering crash as the engine went through the closed doors of the shed and disappeared inside. There were more crashing sounds from inside the shed, a final hiss of steam, and then silence. A few minutes later Conrad walked unsteadily through the shattered doors and began to look around him. With sudden alarm I saw that he was looking thoughtfully at a pick-axe that lay on the ground near him. About the same time as Conrad picked it up, I started to run.

As I shot across the quarry, Conrad followed with the pick-axe cradled in his arms and a look of grim concentration on his face that was positively frightening. For a drunken man he moved with surprising speed, and by the time I had fled from the quarry and was on the last lap to the billet, he was barely a dozen yards behind me. With a final burst of speed I made the compound and, dashing into the billet, slammed the iron doors behind me. I leaned against them, panting, while Conrad roared and banged the pick against the door with frustrated fury. A few minutes later I heard the voices of the guards adding to the general uproar outside. This went on for some time and then there was silence. After allowing a safe interval to elapse, I cautiously opened the doors to find myself facing the grinning guards.

'He's gone,' one of them said. 'But if you want to go back to England, I don't think you'd better go and work in the quarry again.'

Fortunately there were no serious repercussions from this incident, and much later I even went to work in the quarry again. By then even Conrad was slightly amused by what had happened. A tentative suggestion on my part that we should work together again was, however, firmly rejected.

The months went by, and different guards came and went, some better, some worse than the first ones, but generally speaking there was no improvement in the working conditions or in the food.

Quite a number of prisoners in the working party began to develop great running sores on their legs which took months to heal, and then left deep scars. These were the only prisoners allowed to go sick. In the beginning there had been a few abortive attempts to malinger, the very first attempt quickly abandoned with the arrival of the mad Feldwebel wildly flourishing a bayonet. After he had gone, further attempts had been discouraged by an announcement from the factory to the effect that prisoners who did not work were entitled only to the bread ration.

One evening, just after we had returned from work, one

of the guards came in with a cardboard box, silently dumped it on the table, and then walked out again. Someone opened the box. In it were the first letters from home. That night the billet was quieter than it had ever been before.

Soon afterwards it was Christmas. There was no work for us that day, and we spent the morning playing cards, sitting in little groups talking of past Christmases, or merely sitting alone, thinking of our people and our wives, knowing that even at this moment they were preparing the table and thinking of us.

Knowing how sentimental the Germans were over Christmas, we had hoped that the directors of the factory might soften enough for this one day to have given orders for a special meal to be laid on for us. We should have known better. There was the usual bowl of soup, and, as a special concession, we were given the weekly rissole on Christmas Day instead of the Sunday.

Late that afternoon, the directors of the factory sent us over a Christmas-tree. It was a very small Christmas-tree, without any decorations, except for a solitary red candle that was perched precariously on the top of it. The Christmas-tree was handed over with great ceremony by one of the guards, who seemed slightly surprised that we were not overwhelmed with gratitude.

All that day workmen had been laying a cable and fixing coloured bulbs to the branches of the great tree that stood in front of the house where all the directors lived. When darkness came, the power was switched on, and as we all stood in the tiny compound looking at the mass of coloured lights twinkling among the branches, the directors and their families came out of the house and grouped themselves around the tree. The children in the party were pushed forward and began to sing *Heilige Nacht* in thin, piping voices, while the parents watched fondly in the background. When they had finished, there was a delighted spatter of applause

73

from the parents, and then everyone trooped solemnly back into the house. No one bothered to look towards the compound.

Slowly, in twos and threes, we wandered back into the billet. Someone lit the candle on the Christmas-tree, and then we sat down at the tables and talked quietly among ourselves until the light was switched off at the main. After that, we sang carols by the light of the flickering candle, until that, too, went out, when we went to bed.

CHAPTER FIVE

Reawakening

SOON after Christmas a consignment of clothes from the Red Cross arrived, and each man was issued with a new battle-dress, a pair of boots, two pairs of underpants, and two vests. The clothes were issued on a Saturday, and when Sunday morning came we handed in our rags and clogs, washed and shaved more carefully than usual, and then, in our new clothes, strutted out into the compound. The guards were sitting in front of the billet, cleaning their boots, and as we stood there, watching them, we noticed for the first time just how shabby their jackets were, how their trousers bagged at the knee, and how even the shine they were putting on their boots could not cover up the deep cracks in the leather.

'Scruffy-looking lot, aren't they?' someone said.

We all agreed that for members of the Master Race, they did not look much. That morning was the turning-point for all of us.

The old guards were replaced by a Feldwebel and two guards from Saxony, who, surprisingly, enough, seemed genuinely anxious to help us as much as possible. There was no more use of a boot up the backside to make us work, but instead, good-natured finger-wagging and pleas for us to be good chaps and to get on with it. In the past, the loud-speaker had been used only to blast us out of bed with the daily early morning record programme of brass bands, blaring out vigorous and ear-shattering marches. Now it played soft music until late in the evening, while we sat at tables, talking quietly among ourselves, catching up on our mending, playing cards, and generally taking advantage of the fact that the lights were now on for as long as we wanted, instead of being switched off at the main at ten o'clock. The Feldwebel bought us a football, and on the following Sunday we played our first match on the factory field, with the Feldwebel happily acting as referee. Men who were ill were now allowed to stay in the billet without losing rations, and even if there was still no medical attention for them, it was at least a big improvement on the old days. Life had suddenly become quite tolerable.

And then the Red Cross parcels arrived, marking a new era in our lives. Although the parcels varied, a typical parcel contained a quarter-pound packet of tea, a half-pound bar of chocolate, margarine, sugar, soap, biscuits, jam, condensed milk, a bar of Bemax, an apple pudding, a tin of vegetables, and two tins of meat of some sort. In addition, there were fifty cigarettes for each man, or, alternatively, if he was a pipe smoker, a quarter-pound packet of tobacco. On an average, the Red Cross supplied every prisoner in Germany with a parcel once a week for the whole period of his imprisonment; a wonderful achievement that earned them the eternal gratitude of us all.

The function of a Red Cross parcel was to make up for the deficiencies of the German rations and to give us a balanced diet containing all the essential vitamins. In time, the Red Cross parcel became the prisoner's most powerful asset, not only for its immediate value as food but also for what he could buy with it. Going in for barter in a big way, prisoners on working parties used Red Cross items to buy eggs, onions, tomatoes, poultry, pianos, wireless-sets, and even women. To obtain the last item generally meant bribing a guard, a procedure not nearly so difficult as might be imagined, and a state of affairs for which the German Wehrmacht had themselves to blame. A German soldier guarding prisoners was not well off. Rationed to five cigarettes a day, dependent on the factory for food that was nearly as bad as ours, it was not surprising that many of them quite cynically accepted food and cigarettes from prisoners in return for certain favours. As time went on and the economic situation grew worse in Germany, with practically everything being sold at inflated prices on the black market, many of the guards took incredible risks in aiding and abetting prisoners to make contact with women, merely for the sake of a few cigarettes or a bar of soap. But even if the Red Cross parcels were sometimes used to bring us comfort in a way not intended, there was never a time when they did not mean the difference between life and death for any prisoner.

In our new clothes, with a Red Cross parcel under our pillow, and many more in the guards' room, we became dictatorial and arrogant, and the interpreter suddenly found himself overworked, translating our grievances to the Feldwebel. We wanted more freedom. We were *not* going to work overtime, and while we were about it, the directors might look into the matter of that pig's swill they called soup. We were *not* working on meagre rations like that. We were *British* and we had *rights*, even if we were prisoners. Getting into our stride, we wrapped the Geneva Convention around the necks of the guards and factory directors, invoking this clause and that clause to justify our complaints. Nearly every day there was a three-cornered row, with the guards quietly remonstrating in one corner, a foreman and a factory director in the other, and us in the middle, stolid and indifferent and ready to go on strike at any minute, knowing that the guards were too gentle to do anything drastic about it.

Although we did not know it at the time, this attitude was already spreading through all the other British working camps. With dogged persistence, prisoners kept harping on the word 'British' with such an air of superiority and cool assumption that they should be more favoured than prisoners of other nationalities, until in the end the Germans did give the British prisoner preferential treatment. There were certain factors that had helped us, for which we could not directly take the credit—our military history which the Germans respected; the fact that we were Anglo-Saxons, and therefore in their minds the nearest race after the Germans to the pure Aryan, and also the perpetual hope that we would make peace with them to fight against the 'Bolshevik Menace'. British arrogance and the conviction that we were the salt of the earth did the rest.

As the weeks went by, and we received Red Cross parcel after Red Cross parcel, we, who had sworn on our hearts that we would never again waste a scrap of food, not even a crumb, began to get surprisingly finicky, and even began to complain about some of the items in the parcels. It was then that someone had the bright idea of using these unpopular items to bribe the guards and keep them happy. A collection was made on the spot, and Percy, the interpreter, disappeared into the guards' room, carrying a Red Cross parcel stuffed with tins.

A few minutes later Percy returned with the Feldwebel at his heels. We were relieved to see that Percy no longer had the parcel, and that the Feldwebel was beaming. Standing in the doorway, Percy raised his hand for silence.

'The Feldwebel has asked me to thank you all on behalf of himself and his guards,' Percy said. 'I am also supposed to repeat a lot of guff about us all being pawns of the politicians and that really we're all brothers at arms. The important thing is that he has graciously agreed to accept a gift from us every week.' Percy grinned. 'I think from now on things are going to be even better than before.'

The Feldwebel beamed, clicked his heels, and then marched out. We stared after him. It really seemed all a little too easy.

With the guards now in our pay, so to speak, it seemed as if we were all set for an easy time. And for a short period we were. Every Saturday the Feldwebel received his weekly packet, and each week we did less and less, until in the end work in the factory almost came to a standstill. Of course, it was all too good to last. Eventually, the factory owners took action, and the guards were replaced by fresh ones with a Prussian Gefreiter in charge. The Gefreiter was a cartoonist's conception of a Prussian officer, a thick-necked, bull-faced man with close-cropped hair and the manners of a pig. He was also a man not given to much conversation, preferring to use the boot or the rifle butt to emphasize an order.

But we were not unduly worried. In a day or so, there would be a Red Cross parcel issue, and then we would show him who were the real masters. Parcel day came, and, as usual, Percy began to make the weekly collection for the guards.

'Come on, boys,' Percy said. 'Let's have your throwouts. It's been a trying week, but this will put a stop to all the nonsense.'

We all made our contributions, and Percy duly departed for the guards' room next door, triumphantly carrying the Red Cross box in front of him. He was gone a long time. When he finally returned, he was still carrying the Red Cross box.

'He refused it,' Percy said. He seemed stunned.

There was a dead silence as the implications of this began to sink in.

'And that,' Percy said, 'is not the end of it. As from next week, all the contents of Red Cross parcels will be opened on the day we receive them, the excuse being that we're liable to store food up to make an escape.'

'He wouldn't dare do a thing like that,' someone said finally. And we all agreed. He just wouldn't *dare*.

The Gefreiter was only too pleased to show us how wrong we were. On the following Saturday, we were told to line up outside the guards' room and to bring our soup bowls with us. We had almost forgotten the Gefreiter's threat, which had been dismissed as a piece of bluff designed to keep us suitably cowed, and we were therefore a little puzzled about the business of the soup bowls. We were soon enlightened.

As each man entered the guards' room, the Gefreiter cut the strings of a parcel, tipped the lot out on the table, opened the tins, tore open the packets, and finally dumped the lot in one glorious heap in the prisoner's bowl. The prisoner walked out rather unsteadily, carrying his bowl past the horrified gaze of the others outside. Inside the guards' room, the Gefreiter was busily repeating the performance. Not being prepared for anything like this, none of us had any tins or suitable containers in which to put this sad debris of a parcel. The result was that we went back to the billet, sorted everything out and retrieved what we could and then ate the rest.

But the Gefreiter had only just begun. It seemed that he was not very impressed with our claims of rights and the privilege of working less than any other prisoners, and we soon found ourselves working harder than we had ever done before. Every day the Gefreiter and his guards kept up a ceaseless patrol around the factory, rifles unslung, ready to use on any prisoner not working like a demon. Lights out was now at nine o'clock instead of ten, so that we would get a good night's sleep and be fresh for work on the following morning. Sunday football was a thing of the past, and we found ourselves working overtime and doing shift-work on the Sunday—a day that had always been free.

Percy went into the guards' room to protest on behalf of all the men—and for the next few minutes the Gefreiter's voice came through the wall in a steady bellow, telling Percy that we had no rights, that we were all dirt, and that we were lazy lumps who were going to be made to work. There were also frequent references to shooting and death. Percy finally returned looking rather pale, and after that there were no more attempts to make the Gefreiter see reason.

We were eventually rescued from the Gefreiter by a high-ranking officer who made a routine visit to see if we had any complaints of our treatment. We had plenty of complaints, all right, but it was a little difficult to decide whether we should make them. By doing so, we might easily get ourselves into further trouble with the Gefreiter, and to no purpose. However, we decided to take a chance, and Percy began talking. The officer listened attentively and made notes, while the Gefreiter glowered in the background. When it was over, the officer closed his notebook, saluted us punctiliously, looked coldly at the Gefreiter, and then stamped off to the guards' billet with the Gefreiter following agitatedly behind him. The doors closed upon them, and once more we heard the familiar sound of a German voice bellowing in anger. But this time it was not the Gefreiter. The next day the Gefreiter and his guards departed.

In time we had frequent visits from officers, whose sole duty, it seemed, was to go around the working parties to deal with the prisoners' complaints. They would always listen politely, not batting an eyelid at some of our more outrageous demands, or at the shocking lies we sometimes told them about some of the guards. The surprising thing was that they always believed the lies we so blandly told them, and quite often some unfortunate guard, whose only crime had been that he had refused to be bribed, suddenly found himself out of the camp and on his way to the front. The German officer class, it seemed, laboured under the misapprehension that there was some truth to the saying that an Englishman's word is his bond. Maybe there is, under certain circumstances—but not in a prisoner-of-war camp.

The guards that replaced them were much more to our liking. A few days after they arrived, Red Cross parcel day came again, and Percy departed for the guards' billet, carrying the usual weekly box of foodstuffs for the guards. This was duly accepted after some doubt on the part of the guards, quickly dispelled when Percy pointed out that it was the customary thing to accept a weekly gift. Everything was back to normal again.

Soon afterwards, the long months of readjustment finally began to crystallize into a more philosophical acceptance of our lot. With no contact with the outside world to remind us of the past, we thought even less of home than before, making the journey back in time only once a month when the letters from England arrived. Whatever sophistication or culture we had assimilated before the war gradually became overlaid with an almost peasant-like attitude towards life, with our thoughts never far away from food, work, or the weather. The only thing that could be said for us was that we had come to understand each other a little more, and were therefore now able to live together in comparative harmony.

With the Red Cross parcels now a regular thing in our lives, the combines started up again, with men pairing off to share their parcels. This was done to economize on such items as tea, and also to obtain a larger variety of tins, by combining the two parcels. For a reason never clearly understood by either of us, Steve and I went into partnership. Possibly the thing that brought us together was that neither of us had any self-discipline when it came to food. As soon as we received our parcels, we immediately opened them and ate all the chocolate, all the biscuits, one tin of margarine, one tin of jam, two tins of meat, one tin of vegetables, one pudding, and sundry other items; a performance that was always watched with great interest by everyone. What was left went the next day, and for the rest of the week we starved. It was quite some time before Steve and I were able to break ourselves of this habit.

The summer came, and the lice became more active than ever, being joined by a ravenous horde of fleas that descended upon us like a plague. Finally, a delousing machine arrived, a cylindrical, Heath Robinson affair with valves, wheels, and meters sprouting out of it. Our clothes were stuffed into the machine, and while we stood around wrapped in blankets, the German soldier who had come with the machine began twirling some of the wheels. The machine chugged violently and puffed steam for a while, and then ejected our clothes, several sizes smaller than before, but free, we were assured, of lice. A few days later the lice recovered from the shock and were as busy as ever again. In response to an urgent summons, the machine returned, and on its second attempt succeeded in getting rid of the lice. After that we were never bothered with them again.

Then personal parcels began to arrive from home, containing cigarettes, books, and chocolates, and in all seriousness the Germans issued the following pamphlet for all prisoners to send home.

NOTICE

P a r c e l s containing written communications for the receiver and objects, which are prohibited by the way in which they are packed, are intended to be withheld from the control (means of all kinds for facilitating escape) will not be delivered any more.

Prohibited objects are:

Money of all kinds and currencies.

Civil clothing for prisoners of war (interned civil persons excluded) and underclothing (pullovers are allowed).

Badges (brassards) for sanitary personnel sent to persons not entitled to wear them.

Weapons and tools to be used as weapons, large clasp-knives and scissors.

Ammunition and explosives.

Tools which are suitable for facilitating escape and for committing acts of sabotage.

Copying apparatuses, carbon paper, and tracing paper.

Compasses, haversacks (rucksacks), maps, cameras, binoculars, magnifying-glasses.

Electric torches, lighters, match-boxes, matches, wicks, candles.

Spirit, alcohol, and alcoholic drinks.

Solidified methylated spirits, objects which easily catch fire, radiators.

Telephones and apparatuses for transmitting and receiving, and component parts for those.

Medicals of any kind and form, vaseline tubes, ammonia muriate (solid or dissolved).

Fruit juice of any kind, chemicals, acids.

Books and printed matter of doubtful or indecent character, newspapers, books with maps attached to them.

Cigarette-paper and cigar-holders made of paper.

Blank paper of any kind, notebooks, writing-paper, postcards.

Potatoes.

Although the Germans saw nothing funny about this pamphlet, it gave us a glorious vision of our parents receiving it while innocently making up a mixed parcel containing a couple of Mills bombs, a revolver and ammunition, a compass, saws and a telephone. Of course, the list may have been made up by some wag on the German General Staff, but knowing the Germans' complete inability to laugh at themselves, I rather doubt it.

The days went by, the weeks went by, with nothing to distinguish one from the other save the arrival of a personal parcel from home or the memory of a successful skirmish in our perpetual battle against the factory. There was a brief period of wild hope when Russia entered the war, quickly dispelled as the Germans went deeper and deeper into Russia. Winter came. Christmas came, celebrated this time by some awful home-distilled Schnapps bought from the workers. And then it was summer once more. Guards had come and gone, some swines, some not, and for six days in every week we had got up and gone out to work at six in the morning and had returned at six in the evening, done our cooking and then gone to bed. On the seventh day we had played cards, written home, lazed around doing nothing, or read over and over again the only three books we had received so far: Jane Austen's *Emma*, *Lorna Doone*, and *Aylwin*, an incredibly boring Victorian novel by Theodore Watts-Dunton. But nothing had really changed—only ourselves.

But things had a habit of changing suddenly on working parties, and one morning we found ourselves packing our few personal belongings and departing to another cement factory on the other side of Oppeln. No reasons had been given for the move, but we suspected that the directors had finally given us up in despair and were now maliciously inflicting us on their fellow directors at the other factory. We were none too happy at the thought of leaving. A new working party was possibly an adventure, but we were not really looking for adventure. After a great deal of effort, we had at last made life fairly tolerable for ourselves where we were. A new working party meant unknown working conditions, unknown and untested enemies among the foremen of the factory, new guards, a new routine, and new billets, all of which might be far worse than we had now.

When we reached the other factory we found it already occupied by British prisoners. They did not seem very pleased to see us, and when we saw the billets we could understand why. The prisoners were housed in two separate buildings; a tiny building, already crowded to overflowing, and a large, crumbling brick building that looked as if it were going to collapse at any moment. As we were shepherded into the larger building, I looked around it in dismay. It had obviously once been a machine-room of sorts, and there were great gaps in the walls where machinery had been torn out to make room for beds. One piece of machinery still remained, a grotesque lump of rusty iron that rose out of the centre of the floor and then sprouted out in all directions in a conglomeration of pulleys and dangling chains. There were no double-tiered bunks, but only long shelves running along the walls at two levels. It was obvious by the few vacant places on the shelves that once we were installed on them we would all be sleeping practically on top of each other. Two large forms, four benches, and a huge cooking stove completed the furnishings. The floors were black and thick with oil that no scrubbing would ever remove, and over the whole room hung a thick haze of smoke that had its source from the black spirals of smoke rising from the cooking stove.

But we found that the working party had many compensations to make up for the awful billet. There was quite a good library, a large pond in the quarry where one could swim in the summer, and a set of guards whose only desire was to spend most of the day on their bunks smoking our cigarettes. The prisoners who had been there before our arrival had dedicated themselves so successfully to the task of doing nothing that all the foremen had finally capitulated and given most of them jobs minding machinery that did most of the work for them. The rest did more or less as they pleased, generally living in the lavatories for most of the shift.

The months went by quite pleasantly, considering the circumstances. Red Cross parcels continued to be issued every week, and the personal parcels arrived more frequently than ever. Some prisoners received parcels from complete strangers who had been given a name picked out at random by the Red Cross, and after a few of these had arrived, Steve conceived his great plan that was to bring us a little additional comfort for the rest of our days as prisoners.

Steve was a man with a permanent hunger, and therefore found the Red Cross parcels, and the bits and pieces we picked up in barter, quite inadequate for his needs. When the first parcels had arrived from the unknown benefactors, Steve had been wildly hopeful that one of us would also be lucky. When time and no parcel had finally dampened even his boundless optimism, Steve brooded on it for a while and then approached me on the subject.

'I've been thinking about that parcel business,' Steve said. 'I suppose there's no point in us writing to the Red Cross, bringing our names to their attention?'

'No,' I said firmly. 'There isn't.'

'If we were lucky and received a parcel out of it, you could have all the cigarettes and tobacco,' Steve said hopefully.

'For God's sake, Steve,' I said, 'don't be so dim. The Red Cross would only make sure your name was never given after that.'

'There must be some way of getting in the racket,' Steve said. 'I'm going to give some thought to the matter.'

Later that day I found Steve laboriously writing a letter. Looking over his shoulder I saw that it was addressed to a well-known British film actress for whom Steve had often professed the greatest admiration.

'What's the idea, writing to her?' I asked.

'I'm writing a fan-letter,' Steve said calmly.

'Steve,' I said, 'doesn't it strike you that this is hardly the time or the place to be writing a fan-letter? Especially as you're not likely to see a film of hers for a long time.'

'Listen,' Steve said patiently. 'What would you do if you received a sad, sad letter from a P.O.W.?'

'I suppose I'd answer it,' I said doubtfully.

'She'll do more than that,' Steve said. There was a smug expression on his face which I found particularly irritating.

'All right,' I said wearily. 'I'll buy it.'

'This letter,' Steve said, 'contains admiration, respect, and pathos—lots of pathos. In fact, it's very sad. Now, how could a nice woman like —— —— show how touched she was by it? By sending a parcel, of course.' Steve leaned back and gazed dreamily at the ceiling. 'She might even put in a regular order for the duration of the war.'

I looked at Steve with new respect. 'It might work at that, providing you lay it on thick enough. What have you written so far?'

Steve squinted short-sightedly down at the letter before him and then began to read:

'Although it has been a long time since I have seen one of your films (I have been a prisoner since the *very beginning*), I still remember the great pleasure your performances gave me. Tattered and hungry as I am and so very far from the life I once knew, I would still like to know what films you have made in the past few years. If ever I do come back —which is rather doubtful—I shall most certainly want to pick them up.' Steve looked up. 'That's as far as I've got at the moment. Now somehow I've got to work in the grub angle.'

I shuddered. 'Well, it's your name going on the bottom of that letter, not mine.'

'I've no doubt that you'll want your share of the parcels when they come,' Steve said coldly. 'As far as I can see, this has great possibilities. We could send off several like this. Some of them are bound to click.'

Steve finally decided that to start with he would send off only the one letter. Many months later he received a charming letter from the film star, giving him a list of all the films she had made since the beginning of the war. There was, however, no mention of a parcel on the way, and for a long time after that Steve went around talking of how his trust in the kindness of a certain person had been misplaced and how you could never tell a person's character by his face. After that, Steve seemed too disheartened to send out any more letters on the same lines.

Meanwhile, we had decided to start a concert party. Obtaining permission from the Kommandant to use a disused building behind the billet, we began to convert it into a theatre. Using items from our Red Cross parcels to buy materials, we built a stage, prepared a lighting system, complete with dimmers and footlights, and made curtains and scenery. A band was organized, instruments bought, and sketches and music sent out by the Red Cross, obtained from Stalag. Soon afterwards, the usual bedlam of the billet was augmented at odd hours by the discordant strains of the band rehearsing in the next building. At the same time the drama section were also generally rehearsing their lines in a corner of the billet, shouting and bawling to make themselves heard above the din.

Early on in the proceedings it had been decided to call the concert party NENA, an abbreviation of *Nicht Essen, Nicht Arbeit*, the perpetual battle-cry of all prisoners on working parties. For an emblem we made a shield, and painted on it two crossed shovels suspended over a lavatory pan, symbolizing the prisoners' usual place of residence during working hours. We knew that the Kommandant had no illusions regarding our attitude towards work, and we were sure that he would take the joke good-naturedly if he saw the shield and demanded an explanation.

The Kommandant attended one of the rehearsals, saw the shield, and was far from amused. It seemed that the Kommandant had his own interpretation. The shield was a studied insult to Germany. The crossed shovels represented our attitude towards the German economy, and the lavatory pan was supposed to be Germany. The terms in which he actually put it were a little cruder, however. It was an interesting interpretation, and afterwards we came to the conclusion that it was rather a pity we had not thought of it ourselves.

There was a bitter speech from the Kommandant on the ingratitude of British prisoners, who thought they could buy the soul of a German officer for a few cigarettes, which had been accepted only as a token of the good fellowship that could exist between soldiers, irrespective of nationality and wars. But now things were going to be changed. Privileges were going to be stopped. Prisoners were going to work for a change. In fact, everything was going to be very different from now on. The Kommandant stamped out of the building, leaving us to contemplate a rather unpleasant future.

Fortunately, the whole business blew over in a couple of days. When Red Cross parcel day arrived, the Kommandant accepted his cigarettes with cold dignity and then retired to his bunk. After that, everything was as it had always been.

And then something happened that gave us real cause for worry. The Canadians launched their Commando Raid on Dieppe, and a few days later the German newspapers were full of accounts of how the Canadians had manacled their prisoners and then thrown them into the sea when making their escape. The chained bodies of German soldiers had been washed up, exposing to Germany the barbaric way the Allies treated their prisoners. We read the accounts, discussed whether there was any truth in them, and then forgot all about the incident. There were more important things to think about: Red Cross parcels, an interesting business deal for eggs going through, the programme for the next concert party; all the comings and goings of our self-contained lives in which the war no longer played any decisive part.

But we had not heard the last of the Dieppe raid. About a week later the Kommandant informed us that the German High Command had issued an order that British prisoners were to be put in chains, as a reprisal for the Dieppe raid. The Kommandant had no idea as yet how this would affect the working parties. The only thing he knew was that the R.A.F. prisoners in Stalag VIIIB were already in chains.

There was a period of anxious waiting, and then we heard that the order would affect only R.A.F. personnel. Soon afterwards, the Sergeant in charge of the working party made a routine visit to Stalag VIIIB, and returned with the reassuring news that the British prisoners had succeeded in making keys to fit their chains which were now worn only as a piece of rather tiresome equipment when strolling around the camp and for roll-calls. Eventually it dawned on the Germans that their reprisals were not being as effective as they might have been. But by then the excitement over the Dieppe raid had died down, and the chains were removed completely.

After that, nothing disturbed our usual peaceful routine until the Kommandant's daughter arrived one Sunday afternoon, and in the space of a few hours succeeded in completely demoralizing the whole camp. She came into the camp about lunch-time; a dark, pretty girl of about twenty, carrying a small travelling-case. Smiling briefly at the few prisoners lounging around the compound, she disappeared into her father's quarters. The news was passed round of her arrival, and soon everyone was in the compound, hop-

ing to catch a glimpse of her. We were not to be disappointed. When she finally emerged she was dressed in a
scanty red bathing costume, skin tight on the few places it
did cover her. Smiling at the gaping prisoners around
her, she tripped across the compound and made towards the
small piece of waste ground that lay behind the billet. Not
daring to follow, we all rushed inside the billet and fought
for positions at the solitary rear window. Looking through
the window, we saw the Kommandant's daughter going
through a series of languid P.T. exercises which were more
sensuous than athletic. The noise in the billet gradually
grew in volume until it sounded like the zoo at feeding-
time. Still smiling, the Kommandant's daughter continued
with her exercises. Finally, after a series of almost obscene
contortions, she stopped, grinned up at the window, and
then demurely tripped back to Papa's quarters. The whole
performance had been a calculated piece of titillation that
left us unsettled for weeks. Early that evening she left.

Life on that working party had always seemed really
too good to last for any length of time, and for many of us it
suddenly ended with the arrival of a civilian doctor who
descended on the camp without warning, examined every
man carefully, and then informed those that had been
graded A1 that they were being sent to a mine in Poland.

A few days later I was saying good-bye to Steve, who had
been fortunate enough to have had a bad bout of skin
trouble when the doctor had arrived, and was therefore one
of the lucky ones not going. I found Steve on his bunk,
looking steadily at the ceiling.

'Well,' I said, 'I'm off.'

'I know,' Steve said. 'I don't suppose you'll find it as bad
as you think.'

'I don't suppose so,' I said.

'How long have we been together?' Steve said after a
pause.

'Getting on for three years,' I said.

'Oh well,' Steve said. 'I suppose it will all come to an end some day.'

We were silent for a while.

'Well, good-bye, you big oaf,' I said. 'And look after yourself.'

'Good-bye,' Steve said. He dived a hand under his pillow and produced a tin of cigarettes. 'Here, you'd better take these.'

'If you think I'm going to say no, you're mistaken,' I said, sticking the tin in my battle-dress blouse. 'See you after the war,' I said. And then I walked away and joined the others gathering outside.

CHAPTER SIX

The Mines

THE countryside had given way to the large industrial belt around Hindenburg and Beuthen, and now there was only the sight of grim-looking factories, blackened houses, and an occasional glimpse of a squalid street. I looked gloomily out of the railway-carriage window at the forest of belching chimney-stacks, and thought of the cement factory we had left behind us. The billets there had been pretty awful, but the working conditions had been almost the best that any prisoner could hope for in the circumstances. Somehow I had the feeling that it was going to be very different at our new camp.

'Oh, Christ,' someone muttered beside me. 'Just look at it!'

It was certainly a depressing sight. There seemed no end to it as we passed glass-works, iron foundries, chemical works and breweries, and of course the inevitable mines with great slag-heaps rising like miniature mountains to meet the spinning wheels at the tops of the pits. At last the train rattled past Beuthen, and then crossed the border into Poland, where the scenery began to improve a little. Soon after, the train stopped at a town called Sosnowiec, and a few minutes later we were on the station platform being handed over to a new set of guards, who had been waiting there for our arrival. There were hasty good-byes to the old guards, and then we were going through the barrier for our first sight of a Polish town.

The first thing that caught our attention outside the station were the ancient-looking barouches lining the kerb. The cabbies at the reins were all very old men, thin and bent and wearing cockaded hats and black frock-coats that had seen better days. The barouches, the drooping horses between the shafts, and the cabbies themselves, old and dignified-looking, seemed to belong to another age. As we passed, one of the cabbies lifted his hat and bowed to us gravely. There was, however, nothing dignified about the gesture he made to the guards behind their backs.

The elderly man sweeping up the horse manure in the yard was very much more the sort of thing we had expected to see. On his jacket was sewn a large yellow star—the Star of David.

'*Jude*,' said one of the guards, pointing a derisive finger. 'Balls,' someone said. And then we were out of the station and marching in the gutter of the main road.

Although we had anticipated that the Poles would be friendly, we were quite unprepared for the warmth of their welcome. We had only gone a few yards down the road when they began to gather in large crowds on the edge of the pavement; smiling people, who waved and called out and jerked encouraging thumbs in the air with an almost reckless disregard for the guards walking beside us in sullen silence. As we waved back, I could not help thinking how different all this was from the laughter and the jeering voices that had followed us along the main street of Oppeln, and how different these smiling faces were to the still not forgotten hard and bitter faces that had watched us march through Calais as prisoners.

We learnt later that most of the young men from Sosnowiec had been taken away to work as slave-labour in Germany. Apart from key technicians and miners, the population now mostly comprised elderly people, young boys, women, and young girls, who were forced to do heavy labour in the local factories. It was therefore not surprising that a female element was predominant on that afternoon when we walked through Sosnowiec for the first time, and as they waved and smiled at us in a way that we had not seen women smile for years, it struck me that working in Poland might have its compensations. We waved back at the girls, leered at them, and made crude remarks, while the crowds on the pavement grew thicker and more noisy, until in the end our march through the town began to look like the triumphant progress of a liberating army.

But our moment of glory was soon over. The guards, red-faced and distinctly unhappy, hurried us through the town until at last we were out of it, and walking along a country road, completely deserted save for a single tram that went by, its bell ringing with unnecessary violence. Now that we were out of the town, the guards became quite talkative. They told us that the mining camp was in a village called Piaski, some miles away, and that it was a brand-new camp, built to accommodate nearly three hundred prisoners, nearly all of whom had arrived earlier that day from other working parties. Conditions in the camp would be good, but we would have to work hard. We would be issued with mining clothes that night, and tomorrow we would begin work. That last piece of information was enough to make us forget all about those wonderful Polish girls we had seen lining the streets of Sosnowiec.

It was dusk when we arrived at Piaski, a very small village that was nothing more than a cluster of streets grouped around a mine that looked even more awful than any of the mines we had passed in the train. As we walked slowly up the road towards the camp, the few people who were on the pavements stopped to watch us pass; some old men, still in their mining clothes, a couple of youths wearing pit helmets and carrying lamps, and a group of strapping young girls with enormous breasts and coal-dust smeared on their faces.

'No decent German would have anything to do with women like that,' one of the guards said, pointing to them and then spitting. 'They're like animals. All Poles are the same. Like animals. No *kultur*.'

A few minutes later we came to a halt outside the camp itself. It was larger than any other working-party camp I had seen; a series of barracks with a small field behind them, and all of it surrounded by a double row of barbed wire and overlooked by four sentry towers mounted with machine-guns. Although it was only dusk, the whole compound was brilliantly illuminated by great arc lamps that blazed down on it from the four corners of the camp. It was all very different from the cement factory, where there had been a complete lack of discipline, and only some rather futile netting around the compound to keep us in. The guards that watched us from the windows of their barrack looked distinctly unpleasant and brutal types; types who were probably not prepared to be reasonable and co-operative for the price of a few cigarettes. It was all very depressing. We were counted off, the gates swung open, and dismally we trailed into our new home.

But we found that the camp had its compensations. There were three large barracks, each accommodating ninety men, a sick-bay with a British M.O. and two orderlies in charge, a cook-house, a recreation hall, and a small barrack where the British Sergeant and the interpreter lived in solitary splendour. It was the barracks themselves that made up for the grim trappings around the camp. Each barrack was split up into twelve rooms, each room housing eight men. In every room there was a small cooking stove, new blankets, new stools, a new table, white, untrodden boards, a locker for each man, and leaded glass windows that could be left open or shut. After the overcrowded and filthy conditions of the previous working camps I had been in, the cleanliness and the comparative privacy of the rooms seemed positively luxurious.

Within a very short time we were all settled in rooms. Among the seven other men sharing a room with me were three from the very first working party—Tommy, Arthur, and Cyril, who had been a commercial artist in civvy street. As the four of us stood by the window later that evening, we all agreed that perhaps we had not done so badly, after all, by leaving the cement factory. We were fortunate in having one of the best rooms in the camp for seeing something of the outside world. Facing the outside wall of our barrack was the wire, and then a few feet beyond that a row of half-built houses that ended just before they reached the windows of our room. This left us with a clear view of the street that came up to within twenty-five yards of the camp. Directly facing our window was a house. On the steps sat three girls in their early twenties. Idly Cyril waved to them, and immediately one of the girls stood up and waved back.

'Looks like you've made a hit, Cyril,' Tommy commented.

The girl disappeared into the house, and then came out again a few minutes later carrying a piano-accordion. Sitting down on the steps again, she struck some opening chords, and then, looking towards us, the three of them began to sing.

'Well, I must say this is very nice,' I said. 'Very nice indeed. I never thought I'd live to see the day when I was serenaded by a woman. Now, if I didn't know we were going down the mine tomorrow, I could be quite happy at this moment.'

Something thudded against the side of the barrack. Looking out, I saw heads poking cautiously out of some of the other windows.

'What's going on?' I called out.

'Girls!' someone whispered tensely. 'Dozens of them! They're all in those half-built houses opposite. One of them has just chucked a packet over the wire.'

'The guards are going to see this in a minute,' Tommy said gloomily. 'And then there's going to be trouble.'

Standing by one side of the windows, we could just see into the last house. Through the gloom of the oncoming night we could just discern the two figures standing quite still by the window. We could see enough to tell us that they were women all right. Like most of the other Polish women we had seen, they were well built.

A prisoner from one of the other rooms suddenly appeared in front of our window. Whistling casually, he sauntered up and down in front of the wire, ostensibly getting a little air. A guard watched him closely from a sentry tower, and then, satisfied that the prisoner was not up to any mischief, he turned his gaze the other way. In a second the prisoner had darted forward and picked up the packet that was lying on the ground. As he came back into the barrack, we all went out into the passage to meet him.

'What's in it?' I asked.

He unwrapped the parcel. 'Bread,' he said, 'and a note written in Polish. I'll get that translated down the mine to-morrow. Bound to find some Pole who can speak German.'

Slowly we went back into the room. 'A little bread wouldn't come amiss in this room,' I said. 'Especially as we don't know when we're going to get the Red Cross parcels.' As we all went to the window again, another parcel sailed over the wire.

'That one is for me,' I said.

There was a rapid burst of machine-gun fire. As I ducked I had a fleeting vision of spurting earth and jiggling wire as the bullets went through it, and then we were all beneath the window in an undignified heap.

'What about the packet now?' Tommy asked dryly from the floor.

'I don't think I'll bother,' I said.

'You stupid bastards are going to get us all in trouble in here,' a voice said from one of the beds. This was a most unfair remark in the circumstances, but as it came from 'Tiger', a Regular soldier who had promptly told us on our arrival in the room that he had been a boxer in the Army, we kept a discreet silence.

When we rose to our feet, all was quiet again. The girls on the steps had stopped singing as soon as the firing had started. Now, as we reappeared, the piano-accordion had started up again. Keeping a discreet distance from the window, we listened in silence to the sad, plaintive air coming through the growing darkness.

'It's certainly something new to find yourself among civilians who don't treat you like dirt,' Cyril said slowly.

'And among women who don't look at you as if you're only good for a laugh.'

I listened to the young voices singing. 'I think perhaps I preferred it the other way,' I said slowly. 'All this only brings home what we're missing.'

Soon after, the girls waved us good night and then went into the house, and closing the windows we went to bed.

At four-thirty the next morning the guards were clumping down the passage and banging on the doors. Crawling out of bed, we washed and then donned the thin blue cotton jackets, black trousers and pit helmets with which we had been issued almost as soon as we had stepped into the camp. No one spoke a word as we brewed tea. Outside, it was quite dark.

'It's like getting up in the middle of the night,' Arthur said suddenly, almost to himself.

'Shut up!' Tiger snarled at him across the table.

The two of them rose to their feet.

'Oh, for God's sake pack it up,' I said wearily. 'Haven't we got enough to worry about?'

With terrifying speed, Tiger got up and bounded over towards me.

'Did you say something?' he enquired, placing a fist under my nose.

'No,' I said.

After that the room was like a tomb. If nothing else, we learnt a lesson from that brief episode. From then on we made it a rule to say as little as possible at that time in the morning, when a single word could start a row with some-one who had got out of the wrong side of the bed.

At five o'clock we were on parade, and at five-thirty we were standing at the shaft head, lamps in hand and waiting to go down in the cages. Blearily I looked at a woman in trousers who lounged against a wagon, gazing at us with a look in her eyes which I thought was singularly inappropriate for that time of the morning. A few minutes later, I was on my way down for my first day's work in the pit.

At two o'clock in the afternoon I was out of the pit again, shaken and horrified with what I had seen. Inexperienced as I was, it had taken me only the one shift to see that the mine was being worked with a complete disregard for human life. I had seen sweating Poles working desperately and taking all sorts of risks to fulfil a daily quota: I had seen men being forced to work in huge chambers where carbon monoxide was present, and had seen them come out again, violently sick; and I had seen young boys of eight and nine, working on haulage and on most of the other jobs not directly concerned with getting coal from the face. The boys were still below, for only prisoners worked an eight-hour shift. The Poles worked twelve hours daily, seven days a week.

And yet after a few days we were taking it all for granted. We knew that as far as the Germans were concerned, the only important thing was the coal. It had to be got out fast, and if a few lives were lost in the process, well, there were always more Poles or prisoners to take the place of the maimed or dead. We therefore took what steps we could to protect ourselves. We made it a rule never to go near the coal-face if possible, to always pretend that we were quite incapable of using a pick and shovel and were fit only to do the jobs the children were on, and to always keep near the exit to the chamber where we were working. This kept our mortality rate down, but it did not endear us to the Poles, who had had their quota upped as soon as we had joined them, and who thought that as we worked together as comrades, we should also share the work and the risks. Much as we liked the Poles, we could not agree with them.

In time we got to learn the difference between a creaking roof that was only settling and a roof that was going to fall. Quite often the roof did fall, and there was a mad dash for safety while the roof groaned and then finally exploded into a deafening roar as the props collapsed. Afterwards the Poles went back, shored up the roof, put back the props, cleared what stone they could to one side, and then went on working as if nothing had happened. But not always. Sometimes the Poles were a little too slow in getting out, and then someone was either hurt or killed. But never a prisoner. Lounging near the exits, half-heartedly picking up a few lumps of coal, they were always in the best position to be the first out, and they always were.

The one thing we really dreaded was being sent to work in 'the strip', a narrow gallery about six feet high and more than a hundred yards long. Here, scores of men worked on the face in teams, cutting and blasting, and then shovelling the coal on to an ancient conveyor belt that was always breaking down. All through the shift, shouting overseers roamed up and down the gallery, making life hell for everyone. Water seeped through the walls in certain sections, and then ran down the floor to the bottom of the gallery, where it was finally pumped away. Carbon monoxide poisoned the air in other sections, where men worked until they could work no more, and were then replaced by Poles summoned from other faces. All this made 'the strip' a very unpleasant place to work in. What made it a dangerous place were the iron supports that were used to prop up the roof in that part of the mine. These were more modern and more efficient than wooden props, but as they were always hastily erected the roof came down just as often there as anywhere else—and without any of the warning sounds that a good wooden prop gave whenever a roof was on the verge of going.

Every so often the belt would be moved forward and the roof behind it deliberately collapsed to lessen the over-all roof area. This was a terrifying business that meant pulling out the supports and then leaping for safety under the newly propped section. Sometimes the roof stayed where it was for some minutes, and on other occasions it supplied the mine with a few more casualties by coming down before the props were hardly away. All in all, 'the strip' was a place to be avoided at all costs.

The whole camp worked three eight-hour shifts, seven

days a week, with one Sunday off in three. Every week-end we changed shifts by doing what was called a *Roll Schickt*. This meant that on the change-over we did sixteen hours' work out of twenty-four hours; coming out of the pit at our normal time, and then going down again eight hours later to do another shift.

The guards never came down the mine, so the only people we had to contend with below were the *Steigerer*— the armed overseers, who prowled around the mine seeing that everyone was working their guts out for the Greater Germany. The overseers were all *Volksdeutsch*, which meant they were of German parents who had settled in Poland some time before the war. The Germans whose homes and roots were still in Germany looked down on the *Volksdeutsch*. Not fully accepted by the Germans and hated by the Poles, with whom they really had more affinity because of their upbringing in Poland, they lived in an uneasy sort of middle world between the two. As their position always seemed a little precarious, they were servile to the Germans and brutal to the Poles.

The overseer in charge of the section where I was working was a little different; a thin, sensitive-faced man, who had immediately made the mistake of trying to reason the prisoners into working. Despite his mining qualifications, he was also a very simple and gullible man, as I learnt to my advantage one day. Coming upon me working at the face with my customary lack of enthusiasm, he stood there watching for some time.

'You handle that shovel like a woman,' he said finally. 'You should be ashamed of yourself, a fine, strapping fellow like you.'

'I've been used to working with my brains, not my hands,' I said with dignity.

The overseer raised his eyebrows. 'What did you do before the war?' he asked curiously.

I had held a very insignificant clerking post, but I had

no intention of telling him this. Instead I said briefly: 'The Government.'

The overseer looked impressed, so I decided to add a real whopper. More as a joke than anything else, I said casually: 'That's right. One of Churchill's right-hand men. In a minor post, of course.'

I had not really expected him to take me seriously, but to my surprise I saw that he was now looking at me in awe.

'Vincent,' he said, 'you should not be working on the face. We must find something more interesting for you.'

Something more interesting turned out to be a nice cushy job on haulage, delivering pit props to the different sections. That night I told Cyril, Arthur, and Tommy what had happened. The next day Tommy mentioned casually to the overseer that he had been an engineer, Arthur talked airily of the days when he had been a business director with many men under him, and Cyril spoke of his past brilliant career as an artist. Before the shift was over, Tommy was ambling around the mine with the electrician, Arthur was happily sending the wagons up in the cages, and Cyril was working with me on haulage.

It was while Cyril and I were on the haulage job that we had our first spot of real trouble down the mine. We had been given some props to take down to one of the other sections, and having delivered them were pushing the empty wagon back to our own section. Suddenly two Poles came staggering out of a chamber and then collapsed against the wall. They were being violently sick, when an overseer we had never seen before arrived on the scene. He looked coldly at the two retching men and then swung round on us.

'You two,' he snapped, 'take their shovels and get to work in there.'

Cyril and I looked at the two green-faced Poles lying against the wall.

'We're working in number four section,' Cyril said.

'Don't argue,' the overseer shouted. 'I'll see your overseer. Now get in there and start working.'

'I'm not working where there's gas,' I said.

The overseer whipped out his pistol and, moving forward quickly, jammed it in my stomach. 'Now are you going in there to work?'

Trying to ignore the pistol buried in my stomach, I debated the point with Cyril.

'Maybe in the circumstances we should go in,' I said.

'Certainly not,' Cyril said. 'Don't worry about the pistol, he won't shoot.'

'It's all right for you,' I said. 'The pistol's not in your stomach.'

But I knew Cyril was right. He would not shoot. He was only a *Volksdeutsch*, and as such would not dare to override the authority of the military by shooting a prisoner on his own initiative.

'We're not going in,' I told the overseer. 'You can call the guards if you like.' I knew I was fairly safe with that one, as we were some miles from the shaft.

'This is sabotage,' the overseer bellowed. 'Even if I don't shoot you, the guards will have you against the wall for this.'

'Yes, yes,' Cyril said in a mock consoling voice. 'The guards will shoot us.'

I thought that Cyril was now really taking it a bit far, and I began to edge back to the wagon.

'Let's get out of here,' I muttered, 'before there's real trouble.'

Cyril joined me and together we began to move off with the wagon. As a screaming voice followed us down the passage, Cyril said reproachfully: 'You should have been more tactful. Now you've got him so worked up that he's liable to forget what he's doing and shoot.'

I listened to the demented voice of the overseer behind us and shuddered. We had made him look a fool in front of the two Poles, and the only way he could really erase that from their minds was to shoot us. But he did not shoot us, and a few moments later we heard him bellowing at the Poles telling them to get back to their work. Looking back we saw the two Poles stagger to their feet and disappear into the chamber again.

At the end of the shift there was more trouble. Reaching the shaft we found the rest of the prisoners due to go up in the cages surrounded by a crowd of angry overseers. I had never seen so many overseers together at one time. One angry overseer in full blast was always a sight worth watching, providing you were not the victim, but the sight of this wildly gesticulating bunch of red-faced men, alternately shouting at each other and then at the prisoners, was really more amusing than frightening.

'What's going on?' I asked as we joined the others.

'We're on strike,' someone growled. 'These bastards want us to go back and do another four hours' work. You know what that means. They're trying to get us to do a twelve-hour shift, like the Poles.'

'Getting a bit hectic these days, isn't it?' Cyril murmured, as we joined the others.

'Oh well,' I said. 'We've been letting them get away with too much for too long, anyway.'

The shouting continued, and then when the overseers saw that they were getting nowhere the pistols came out. There was more shouting, more threats, more pistol waving, a lot of Anglo-Saxon words from the British, and then, finally, a call on the phone to the guards to come down and deal with the problem. But it seemed that the guards were not very keen on coming down the mine. The phone crackled as we listened tensely. Could not the overseers deal with the matter themselves? No, the overseers could not deal with the matter themselves. Soldiers were needed to put these swine in their places.

The guards arrived with fixed bayonets and, stepping rather reluctantly out of the cage, came forward. The conversation between ourselves and the guards started quietly enough, with the Gefreiter in charge suggesting with cunning reasonableness that we should get back to work while he went and straightened things out with the Kommandant, who would, no doubt, have us out of the pit within the hour. As we knew that the overseers would never have tried keeping us down there without the Kommandant's consent, the answer to that was a flat no. The Gefreiter grew more aggressive. Had we forgotten that we were prisoners, and therefore would work whatever hours we were told to work? To that we trotted out the usual business of the Geneva Convention, and a new one calculated to bring the guards down on our side: that we were not only prisoners, but soldiers, like themselves, not slaves. But the Gefreiter was unimpressed. After that negotiations broke down completely and things began to get out of hand. The guards unslung their rifles, the Gefreiter's pistol appeared in his hand, a shot was fired into the roof, and the guards and overseers blended their voices in a bellowing chorus of intimidation. While all this was going on we looked blankly into space, lit cigarettes and puffed at them nonchalantly, and generally behaved as if there were no one there but ourselves. Everything grew silent again. The guards hesitated. I suppose they knew that they could not very well shoot the lot of us. The Gefreiter muttered something to the overseers, and then rushed into one of the cages, presumably on his way to phone the Kommandant for instructions.

When the Gefreiter came down again, we nerved ourselves to face the final showdown, expecting real trouble this time. But there was no trouble. Instead, the Gefreiter sullenly told us to get into the cages. The overseers began to protest and were rudely silenced by the Gefreiter, and then we were in the cages and on our way to the surface. And that was the last we heard of having to do a twelve-hour shift.

We could think of only one reason for our having been allowed to get away with it. The Kommandant and the mining directors must have cooked up the idea between themselves, with, no doubt, a discreet arrangement between both parties for the Kommandant to be recompensed suitably for his co-operation. When we had gone on strike, the Kommandant had not dared to make an issue out of it for fear that the matter might reach the ears of the German military authorities, who would promptly have clapped him in jail, or worse still, as far as he was concerned, sent him to the Russian Front.

The one thing that made working in the mines tolerable, even worth-while in some respects, were the friendships that we struck up with some of the Poles. Most of them were elderly and kindly men, who had spent most of their working life down the one mine. Once they had finally accepted the fact that we were a dead loss as far as work was concerned, we got on with them very well indeed. In the long waits between the cutting and the blasting, we would squat down with them and converse in a mixture of Polish, German, and violent sign language.

Talking to the Poles, we were able to build up a picture of life in and around Sosnowiec under the Germans. It was a grim picture of people living on the edge of death most of the time; of civilians being picked off the streets at random and then strung up from the lamp-posts as a reprisal for some act of sabotage or the killing of a German by the Partisans; of German police constantly descending on whole streets in search of arms and ammunition, indiscriminately shooting or beating up anyone who was suspected of being a 'bandit'; of mass deportations of slave-labour to Germany and people taken off to the concentration camps and never seen again; the familiar pattern, in fact, of all the German-occupied countries. All the Poles who worked with us were frightened that one day they, too, would be taken away, and it was therefore not surprising that they all worked like demons and were careful not to get on the wrong side of the overseers.

The basic food rations for the Poles were poor, and they all supplemented their rations by making weekly trips to Cracow to buy their food off the black market, or by going to lonely farms to buy farm produce. All this was, of course, strictly forbidden, and there were heavy penalties for anyone caught smuggling food. But the Poles did not seem to have much trouble in getting food through, and as soon as we knew that they could lay their hands on a plentiful supply of eggs, onions, tomatoes, and chickens, we wasted no time in getting down to some hard bargaining.

We found that the Poles were interested only in buying cigarettes and woollen goods. Cigarettes were out as far as we were concerned, but as almost everyone had managed to accumulate a plentiful supply of clothing from personal parcels, we were soon flooding the market with pullovers, socks, and balaclavas, which the Poles unravelled and then sold as skeins of wool at a fancy price on the black market. The Poles were as shrewd as we were when it came to business, and there were long and complicated haggling sessions over a single item of clothing that often lasted for days before ending on a satisfactory note for both parties. Actually, the prices we got for our clothing secretly rather staggered us. A pullover, for instance, fetched as much as fifty eggs, a small chicken, and several pounds of tomatoes and onions. Until the Kommandant tumbled to the fact that we were smuggling food into the camp, we were probably living far better than our own people in England.

The first search was a major disaster that yielded up to the Kommandant a great harvest of eggs, poultry, and tomatoes that went straight into the guards' kitchen, and left us glumly contemplating the prospect of having to exist almost entirely on our Red Cross parcels. There had been a time, of course, when a Red Cross parcel had seemed the pinnacle of high living. But we had been spoilt. Fried luncheon roll and Irish stew seemed rather a come-down in the world after a regular diet of fried eggs, omelettes, and succulent chickens. But the Kommandant was no fool. Not wishing to dry up this unexpected source of additional food for himself and his guards, he was careful to see that the searches did not occur often enough to discourage us from attempting to smuggle food into the camp.

But although we were still able to get most of our con-

traband into the camp, we still found it irksome to see some
of it occasionally disappearing into the German barrack to
feed a racketeering Kommandant and a number of guards
whose only interest in life was to make ours as unpleasant as
possible; doubly so, as we knew that the German military
authorities had laid it down that all contraband taken from
prisoners should be given to the nearest hospital. In the end,
we decided that as the local hospital was getting nothing
out of it, we could at least see to it that the Kommandant was
deprived of the bountiful supply of eggs that always con-
stituted the main portion of his haul each time there was a
search.

As it happened, I was on the returning shift when the
next search occurred. As usual, when a search was in the
offing the Kommandant was waiting for us; a lean, sprightly
looking man with glasses, who looked more like a school-
master than a soldier. Standing ready to help him in the
good work of stocking up their larder at our expense was a
vulpine-looking guard and our old friend the Gefreiter. As
we came to a halt, the Kommandant ran an appraising eye
down the column, noting the bulging battle-dress blouses
and slung haversacks that had been bought for the express
purpose of smuggling food into the camp. He smiled sourly,
and said something to the Gefreiter and the soldier. Together, the three of them moved forward.

Stopping in front of Arthur, who was at the head of the
column, the Kommandant placed his hand on Arthur's
haversack, feeling what was inside it with an exaggeratedly
thoughtful expression on his face.

'Eggs!' said the Kommandant finally, in mock surprise.

Behind him the Gefreiter and the soldier cackled dutifully.

'We Germans like eggs,' said the Kommandant, smiling.
He bowed to Arthur with mock politeness. 'Your bag,
please.'

Arthur lifted his haversack from his shoulder, held it
delicately suspended from one finger for a moment, and

then dropped it. The smile vanished from the Kommandant's face. Stooping down, he picked up the bag and opened it. Standing just behind, Arthur and I had a brief glimpse of broken eggshells swimming in yellow yolk.

'So,' said the Kommandant tightly.'Some English humour. You will be punished. . . .' With a slightly glazed look on his face, the Kommandant stopped in mid speech to watch an egg sail skywards from the column.

Almost before the egg had landed everyone who had been carrying eggs dropped them. There was an odd moment of silence, and then with an unearthly scream the Kommandant moved, followed by the Gefreiter and the soldier. With much cursing, the three of them worked their way down the column, booting and cuffing everybody. After that they worked from the bottom of the column back to the top again, repeating the performance.

Beyond that there was not really much the Kommandant could do. The Kommandant bawled threats of solitary confinement in the *bunker*, but we knew that this would not be carried out. There were over seventy of us, and our enforced absence would only bring the Kommandant a sharp note from the directors. That was something that the Kommandant would not want to happen. He was frightened of the directors. Still screaming, the Kommandant ordered the gates to be opened, and we fled inside. The Gefreiter and the guard had gone back to look at the broken eggs that spattered the roadway. They looked genuinely shocked at such waste.

After that it was war to the knife as far as the Kommandant was concerned. He was no longer interested in extra food for himself and his guards, only in seeing that we got nothing into the camp. As the three shifts returned each day, the Kommandant would be waiting to conduct a vigorous search. Nothing got past him, and in the end we gave up trying to get food into the camp.

But the Kommandant had not reckoned with some of the highly inventive minds that were in the camp, and soon after he had instituted his thrice daily searches, a select gathering was invited into one of the rooms to see a demonstration of how to get eggs past the guards. The demonstrator stood in the middle of the room and assured us that there were five eggs on his person. We walked all round him, saw no bulges, and then ran our hands over the usual places where the guards searched. We stepped back again, admitting that there did not seem to be a single egg on him. Rather self-consciously, the demonstrator dropped his trousers to reveal a number of condoms hanging from a piece of string tied round his waist. An egg had been neatly broken into each contraceptive, and now lay neatly at the bottom, making only the slightest bulge. The general effect was rather odd.

A few prisoners adopted this idea and bought contraceptives from mystified Poles, but the idea never really caught on. A few weeks later, the Kommandant and his guards were replaced by another Kommandant, who was quite content to let us do almost what we liked so long as we made no trouble down the mines and did not try to escape. We were in business again.

But we still had one or two problems to resolve, and high on the priority list for attention was our mounting sexual hunger. In the very beginning sex had not presented any problem at all. Lack of food, lack of clothing, twelve hours a day manual labour, and a constant preoccupation with self-preservation had made the sexual act suddenly seem one of the more unimportant things of life. Later, when conditions had improved generally, we naturally amended our views. But the problem, as such, was then partially resolved by our refusal to face up to certain things. With no women around us to use as images for our sexual fantasies, we tended to think of our girl friends and wives. But to think of them in connection with the sex act, also meant having to face up to the fact that they were human—and therefore possibly unfaithful. It was not a thing one wanted to think about in the early hours of the morning, and the fantasies in which we indulged were therefore mostly of a purely romantic type. Like George du Maurier's *Peter Ibbetson*, we used the night and our dreams to step out of our prison to freedom, and meetings that were always idyllic and seldom sullied by sex. This Romanticist's conception of love helped a little to sublimate the more basic instincts.

But now it was rather different. The girls who had first greeted us from the half-built houses outside the camp, gathered nightly in the houses to throw love-letters over the wire to whichever prisoner had taken their fancy. It was all very flattering—and very disturbing. The girls were provocative and tantalizingly near, and each night the men waved to them from the windows, signalled to them in sign language, went out of the hut discreetly to pick up their love-letters, and then went to bed, tormented.

The guards were equally as trigger happy as the others had been, and almost every night the comparative quiet of the camp was shattered by a sudden burst of machine-gun fire that ploughed up the earth in front of the wire, as a badly thrown paper-wrapped stone crashed against the barrack or rattled the wire. As it happened, no one was ever hurt. The girls kept in the safety of those half-built houses, tossing their messages over the wire from the doorways and windows. If they fell near the wire, we made a point of leaving them there. No love-letter was worth the risk of being riddled with bullets.

The three girls in the house opposite were on their step every night, sometimes singing and playing to us, sometimes just sitting there, gazing steadily towards our window. Long after the lights in the barrack-rooms had been switched off, I would often stand by the window, looking across at the now deserted doorstep and at the lights on in the rooms of the house, until they went out and there was only the floodlit wire to study; every barbed hook, twist, and loop of that particular portion now familiar after weeks of bitter contemplation.

On other nights there were sleepless hours of lying in bed

puffing at one cigarette after another and listening to the sounds of the camp; the occasional cough of a guard in one of the sentry towers; the sudden unintelligible babble of someone talking in his sleep in a nearby room; the bubblings, snores, groans, and sighs of my own room mates, and just before dawn the crunch of gravel beneath the boots of a guard walking past to relieve one of the sentries.

A few found an unexpected answer to the sex problem when some of the youths down the mine indicated that they were prepared to prostitute themselves for a few cigarettes. Homosexuality was not so common an occurrence as it might be thought in the circumstances. There had been no evidence of it on my other working parties, and by all accounts it was rare on all working parties. Genuine 'queers' seemed few and far between, and the man who was inclined to drift towards perversion merely as an outlet must have found himself faced, not only with lack of privacy but also with the difficulty of breaking down the barrier of a normal relationship that had been previously established between himself and some other person. The youths in the mine solved the problem for him nicely. The act was done with a stranger, in the dark privacy of the mine, and afterwards he could even speak of it to his friends as a rather amusing and daring experiment. His friends would be mildly shocked and then amused. After all, it was not quite the same thing with a foreigner, was it? When two men were caught in the act in the camp, it was some of the people who shrugged their shoulders at what happened down the mine who were the most contemptuous and loud in their condemnations.

Soon after, the murder of a *Volksdeutsch* overseer gave us something far more serious than our sex problems to think about. The murder, or the execution, as the Poles preferred to call it, was carried out with a casual brutality that seemed to appeal to the Poles, who told us about it on the shift following the night of the murder. Shortly after dark the overseer's little daughter had opened the door to a quietly spoken stranger, who had asked if he might have a few words with her father. The child had gone to the back of the house to fetch her father, and a few moments later the overseer had come to the door—and had been met by a volley of bullets poured into his stomach. By the time the hysterical wife and the crying child had reached the door, the stranger had vanished into the night, leaving the overseer lying dead in a pool of blood in the passageway.

The Poles seemed to relish the fact that the murder had been committed almost in front of the overseer's wife and child, and that the child herself had been indirectly responsible for her father's death. Charming as the Poles were, they were implacable in their hatred for the Germans and for anything or anybody connected with them.

But although the overseer had been one of the most hated men down the mine, the Poles should have known enough about reprisals to know that the murder was not a matter for the general jubilation that went on among them during that shift. Even as we discussed the murder, things had already begun to happen in the village above.

As soon as we came up from the shift, we knew that there was something wrong. The guards seemed rattled and more impatient than usual to get us away from the mine and back to the camp, and as we were bustled through the streets, we saw the reason why. The whole village was swarming with Gestapo and police; the Gestapo sitting silent and bored-looking in their cars, while the police moved in on the houses, shouting and banging on the doors until they were opened by frightened-faced Poles who were immediately hustled back into the passage at the point of a gun.

As the guards hurried us on, a Pole, his face spattered with blood, was brought out of one of the houses and dragged towards one of the waiting cars. A woman followed him as far as the kerb, and stood there moaning and beating her breast in anguish. Almost at the same moment, two more Poles were brought out of another house, unmarked but ashen-faced and trembling as they stumbled past us, handcuffed between two beefy policemen. Farther on there were more cars, more policemen, more Poles being dragged along the pavements, and then at last we were being pushed through the camp gates by the guards, who didn't even bother about the usual count in their anxiety to get us off the streets.

The Poles that were taken away that day never came back, and for quite some time afterwards we thought a little less often of women and food and barter and how best we could twist the Poles, and a little more of what it meant to live under the Germans. The incident brought home what would happen if we lost the war; not an honourable peace and a quiet return to our own homes, but a life of semi-slavery and fear. It was a sobering thought. It may seem surprising that this had not occurred to us before, but, protected as we were to a certain extent by the Geneva Convention, and treated fairly well by the Germans, who still had hopes of an Anglo-German alliance against the Russians, we were apt to blame the occasional shortcomings in our treatment on individuals rather than on the State. In the face of our own treatment, the stories of reprisals, concentration camps, and mass extermination had seemed rather unreal. But not any more.

As Christmas began to draw near, vast quantities of Schnapps were bought and stocked up in readiness to celebrate the occasion. The Schnapps came in two forms of dynamite: the branded bottle, 90 per cent. alcohol and guaranteed to knock you flat on half a bottle, and the home-brewed variety, which sometimes had the most spectacular effects on the unwary. The 'home brew' was liable to reduce one to a state bordering on raving hysteria, but as it was cheaper we generally bought it in preference to the branded variety. It was not until two men on a nearby working party had become blind as a result of drinking home-distilled Schnapps that we took warning and changed our allegiance to the branded bottle.

Christmas came, and began quietly enough with everyone rising late on the Christmas morning and then going off to collect a special Red Cross parcel containing a Christmas pudding, a Christmas cake, a tin of roast pork and stuffing, and various other delicacies appropriate to the occasion. These particular parcels had been sent out from England in the August so as to arrive in good time for Christmas, and were just another example of how the Red Cross organization was doing everything in its power to make our life as pleasant and comfortable as possible.

After lunch the drinking began. In addition to the dozens of bottles of Schnapps in the camp, there were also the barrels of beer which the Kommandant had allowed us to buy as a special concession for Christmas. As these had been bought weeks before and immediately doctored with raisins and yeast, the beer was now well on the way to rivalling the Schnapps in potency. What with the Schnapps, the barrels of beer, bottles of vodka bought by a few connoisseurs, plus the odd bottles of wine, there was enough booze in the camp to start up a fair-sized off-licence.

The drinking went on all through the day and late into the evening. Finally, everyone began to congregate in the main hall, where the camp band had settled down to play some of the latest dance hits that had been sent out to us from Stalag VIIIB. While the band blared out number after number, the prisoners, most of them now very much the worse for wear, stood around in large groups, bellowing out the choruses. In the middle of the hall a number of individualists were going their own way with a spirited performance of 'Knees Up, Mother Brown', much to the annoyance of a few dancing couples, threading their way through the crowds with the grim concentration of people who take their dancing seriously.

Not being a person who gets a great deal of pleasure out of drinking, I had not wasted any cigarettes or clothing on Schnapps. I was therefore cold sober as I stood by the doorway, watching the festivities reach their height. The band's playing became more noisy than before, the singing more and more incoherent, and the 'Knees Up, Mother Brown' squad seemingly more determined than ever to stamp their way through the floorboards. Feeling rather sorry that I was incapable of whipping up enough enthusiasm to join in the celebrations, I retreated before the barrage of sound and went outside.

There was a heavy frost on the ground, and as I stood there gratefully breathing in the cold air, I looked at the hoar-covered wire glistening under the arc lights, and wondered how many more Christmas days like this there would be before the end came. Faintly, from the German barracks, came the sound of the guards singing *'Es geht alles vorüber, es geht alles vorbei,'* a popular German dance number at that time. Behind me, the door swung open and a figure lurched out of the hall, cannoned against me, and then staggered off to be sick in a corner. Slowly I began to make my way through the camp towards my own barrack. As I went past one of the sentry towers, the guard leaned over and called out.

'Fröhliche Weihnachten.'

'Fröhliche Weihnachten,' I said quietly.

Merry Christmas today and a bayonet up the arse to-morrow. Strange people, the Germans.

The barrack-room was empty save for Cyril, who was sitting up in bed, puffing furiously at a cigarette and gloomily surveying the empty Schnapps bottles left lying around from the afternoon party.

'Hallo, Cyril,' I said. 'Not celebrating with the others?'

'You tell me what there is to celebrate,' Cyril said morosely.

As Cyril was obviously in no mood for conversation, I quietly undressed and then clambered into my bunk. I was just settling down between the blankets when the door opened, and The Weasel came into the room.

The Weasel was generally considered to be one of the more harmless guards; officious and a stickler for red tape,

but not given to active bullying. The Weasel walked unsteadily into the middle of the room, and then came to a
halt. Rocking gently on his heels he looked with slightly pro-
tuberant eyes at the Schnapps bottles lying around on the
floor.

'This room is filthy,' The Weasel said thickly. 'Filthy. It
must be cleaned up at once.' He looked at Cyril. 'Who is in
charge here?'

'He is,' Cyril said, pointing to me, and then promptly
disappearing beneath the bedclothes.

Of course, no one was in charge of the room, as I tried to
explain to The Weasel. But The Weasel did not even listen.

'Don't argue,' The Weasel said loudly. 'Get out of bed
and clean up this room.'

'You clean it up,' I said, settling down in the bed again.

This was no doubt rather a silly and somewhat reckless
attitude to take, but I was tired and depressed and in no
mood for an officious and drunken guard. Anyway, I was
sure that I was quite safe. The Weasel had never been
known to raise a finger against a prisoner.

There was a complete silence for a few moments, and
then something prodded me gently in the back. Lifting my
head off the pillow, I turned irritably—and found myself
looking down the barrel of The Weasel's pistol.

'Get out of bed,' The Weasel said, 'or I shoot.'

Whatever The Weasel had against me at that moment,
he certainly could not have complained of any lack of speed
on my part in getting out of bed. Feeling rather alarmed, I
faced The Weasel, conscious that I was rather hampered in
handling the situation by being in my shirt-tails.

'For Christ's sake, Cyril,' I said, still keeping a wary eye
on The Weasel. 'This basket really is drunk. You'd better
get up and give me some help.'

A very large and phoney snore came from the bunk. It
was clear that I was not going to get any help from Cyril.

The Weasel poked his pistol in my stomach and held it

there, his finger trembling on the trigger. 'Filthy English swine should be shot,' he shouted. 'Especially English swine who do not obey orders.'

'No, no,' I said, smiling falsely. 'We are all comrades. This is Christmas. We must forget the war.' Although suddenly feeling very sick, I managed to keep the smile nailed on my lips. I could have saved myself the trouble. My friendly, slightly apologetic smile was completely wasted on The Weasel.

'Silence, you English lump!' he roared, pushing his face closer to mine. 'Silence, or I shoot.'

Even if the light of madness that was now in The Weasel's eyes had not been enough to tell me that he had been on home-brewed hooch, the methylated-spirit fumes he was breathing on me would have been quite enough. Even at that critical moment, I could not help marvelling how the stuff was capable of changing the most harmless men into dangerous maniacs. The Weasel, who would never have drawn a pistol on a prisoner under any circumstances, was just itching to pull the trigger. I had to do something, and quickly. Thinking desperately, I suddenly remembered that Arthur still had a bottle of Schnapps untouched in the cupboard. If I could get The Weasel started on it, I might be able quickly to reduce him to a state of sodden unconsciousness before he did any real harm. It was a slim chance, but about the only one left.

'What you need is a drink,' I said to The Weasel. 'In fact, we both need one. Now, I happen to have some very fine Schnapps in the cupboard. . . .'

Taking a deep breath, I deliberately turned my back on The Weasel and went over to the cupboard. Taking the bottle of Schnapps out of it, I held it towards The Weasel. 'Now let's forget our quarrels and have a drink,' I said.

The Weasel seemed to hesitate. Pulling the cork out of the bottle, I held it under his nose. 'Best quality,' I said.

The Weasel's long, thin, and red nose, which had earned

him his nickname, twitched slightly. 'Schnapps is verboten for prisoners,' he growled.

'But not for guards,' I said.

This time The Weasel didn't hesitate. Snatching the bottle from me, he put it to his lips and tilted his head backwards. I watched with interest his Adam's apple working as the fiery liquid poured down his throat. Finally The Weasel lowered the bottle and looked at me with bloodshot eyes.

'Now you,' he said suddenly, holding out the bottle.

This was an unexpected development. I had hoped that The Weasel would finish off the bottle at one go and then fall flat on his face. I had certainly not expected to be involved in a boozing session. Taking the bottle from him, I took a cautious swig from it. After that we kept passing the bottle backwards and forwards to each other until it was empty. Never having acquired a taste for methylated spirits, I was by then beginning to feel distinctly ill and well on the way to being in the same state as The Weasel. The Weasel, I was sorry to see, was still on his feet and looking as if he could dispose of another bottle without too much trouble.

But my real worries were over. Already The Weasel was putting away his pistol which he had kept in his hand all the time we had been drinking together.

'Comrade,' The Weasel said emotionally. 'My good English comrade.' It seemed that Arthur's bottle of Schnapps had not been wasted after all.

'You're a good Englishman,' The Weasel said, placing an affectionate arm around my shoulder.

'And you're a good guard,' I said.

The Weasel nodded as if satisfied, and then, breaking away from me, he tottered out of the room. I listened to him stumbling down the passage, and then turned to watch Cyril emerging from beneath the bedclothes.

'That's the second time you've left me with a pistol stuck in my stomach,' I said bitterly.

'Someone had to deal with him,' Cyril said. 'And you know the language better than I do.'

'He might have shot me,' I said indignantly.

'Nonsense,' Cyril said.

When Arthur came back later that night and found his bottle of Schnapps gone, he was equally unsympathetic.

'You now owe me fifty cigarettes,' he said coldly. 'You can pay me out of your next parcel from home.'

Soon after, I went out into the washroom next door and was violently sick. In one way and another it had not been a very successful Christmas.

CHAPTER SEVEN

The Art of Going Sick

BEFORE we had been transferred to the mines, the business of going sick had been a fairly straightforward matter, even if not always successful. Having decided that the time had come to have a rest from work, you waited until a particularly cold day arrived. Then, as the guard came in to send you out to work in the early hours of the morning, you would lift your head feebly from the pillow, croak out that you were sick, and then fall back on your pillow and wait to see what happened next.

Things then progressed according to the temperament of the guard responsible for getting the men to work that morning. If he was tough and sensible, he would promptly pull you out of bed, kick you up the backside and start roaring. On those occasions you philosophically went to work. If, on the other hand, he was new or uncertain of himself, you pressed home the point of your sickness as dramatically as possible until you won the day. It often worked quite well. The only unfortunate thing about this system was that, with no M.O. around, you were likely to be sent to work even if you were genuinely sick.

In the mining camp, going sick became a much more complicated matter. Every mining camp had been allotted an English M.O. and a couple of orderlies to attend to the constant flow of prisoners returning injured or maimed from the pits. This meant that whenever you wanted to malinger, you had to pull the wool over the eyes of a qualified M.O., whose main concern was to keep the percentage of sick down so that the genuinely ill would not be driven out to work to make up the daily quota of manpower required. If a sick call was beneath the quota allowed, the officer and his medical orderlies were quick enough to build it up with false cases. As they always kept a roster, it was a very fair way to work.

But waiting for one's turn on the roster was a slow business, and as the work in the pits was unpleasant, to say the least of it, everyone did everything in his power to be ill as often as possible and for as long as possible. In the beginning, the doctor and his orderlies were more than a match for us, and conversations in the sick-bay would go somewhat as follows:

'Well, what's the trouble this time?'

'I've got a pain, sir.'

'What sort of pain?'

'An awful pain in my back, sir. Every time I lift a shovel or bend down, it's sheer agony.'

'Is this where the pain is?' A finger taps the back lightly.

'Aaaaah!' And then a little breathlessly: 'That's it, sir. You've got it right on the spot.'

The doctor and the patient gaze blandly at each other.

'Bring the heat-box, orderly.'

As the medical orderly moves forward with the heat-box, the patient knows that his attempt has failed. The heat-box is a home-made, wooden contraption, semicircular in shape, so that it can be strapped around any portion of a patient's body. Fitted inside it are a number of electric-light bulbs. The so-called therapeutic value of the heat-box is that the radiation from the bulbs will help to ease the patient's pain. It is, of course, quite useless, and both patient and doctor know that it is. The patient goes through the polite make-believe of having treatment, and is then sent off to work. The heat-box is used for rheumatism, vague pains in the legs, and any other complaints cooked up by the prisoners and not possible to diagnose.

After a while we became seasoned troupers in the medical-room skirmishes, and soon became capable of holding our own with the doctor. Gradually, one built up one's own particular technique, based on certain discovered facts.

For instance, it was discovered that smoking a cigarette made from tea-leaves accelerated the heart, as did crushed saccharine. To make doubly sure of the efficacy of this, I used to roll a cigarette filled with tea-leaves *and* crushed saccharine. Having smoked it, I would then run all the way to the medical ward, and once in the queue, hold my breath for long periods while I thought of the most dire things happening to me. By the time I was inside the room, facing the M.O., my heart was pounding and giving the most alarming jumps.

The first time I did this, I was immediately sent to the sick-bay. Smugly, I went back to my room, collected my blankets, and with an airy wave to my room mates, departed for what I hoped was a nice long rest. As we were able to smoke in the ward, I was able to keep myself there for the best part of two weeks. Finally, the officer came round early, before I had had time to prepare a cigarette, with the result that I was immediately discharged.

Another technique employed by the more ambitious prisoners wishing to get back to Stalag was the swallowing of small pieces of silver paper. This was supposed to show up like a stomach ulcer under an X-ray.

Working in the mines got on the nerves of some of the prisoners so much that they were prepared to do almost anything to get out of them. In the end a number of prisoners were cutting off their little fingers so that they would be sent back. This worked very well for some time, until there were so many so-called 'casualties' of this sort, that the Germans no longer sent them back to Stalag, but instead kept them in the local hospital until their wounds had healed and then sent them back to the mines again.

Another favourite trick was worked with the pit wagons. This involved standing on the track with one's body free from the wagon, but with one bent arm still holding it. Another prisoner would then take a flying run with another truck, sending it hurtling down the track at top speed, until it crashed into the prisoner's bent elbow. This was almost guaranteed to give a compound fracture.

An Australian did a thriving trade in smashing the hands of the more squeamish prisoners unable to do the job for themselves. In all the barrack-rooms were a number of three-legged stools with detachable legs. One of these legs brought down smartly across a hand was enough to smash a few small bones, or at least damage the hand sufficiently for the person at the receiving end to have a severely bruised hand that would keep him from work for several weeks.

Some of the more enterprising prisoners thought up some rather original schemes for getting out of the mines. There was, for instance, the case of Cyril's circumcision, an idea that germinated in the mind of Spot Read, a Regular Army man who had been with us on the second cement factory working party and was now sharing the room with the rest of us.

Like all of us, Cyril wanted to get out of the mines, and like all of us, he had gone to the M.O. with a variety of complaints, which had they been genuine would have qualified him for a coffin, let alone being sent back to Stalag. Apart from being grudgingly granted an odd day off here and there, Cyril had not been particularly successful with the M.O., who was never really impressed by anything except a broken limb or some gaping mutilation.

The birth of Spot's idea came by accident, like most great ideas do. We were all sitting around the table one Sunday morning, wondering what to do with ourselves, when Cyril broke the silence.

'I've been getting some slight twinges,' Cyril said. 'And in rather an unusual place.'

Spot looked up with interest. 'Where?'

Cyril told him.

'Well,' Spot said jocularly, 'I shouldn't think you've got anything to worry about, not with the sort of life we've been leading over the past four years.'

The subject was then dropped and we fell silent again.

Spot seemed to be pondering about something. Finally he said: 'You know, Cyril, I think we'd better have an examination.'

Cyril got up in alarm and Spot made a tut-tutting sound of annoyance.

'Don't be a fool, Cyril. You may have something here that's worth plugging to get yourself back to Stalag.'

'Of course I haven't,' Cyril said irritably. He seemed anxious now to drop the subject as quickly as possible.

'I'm the best judge of that,' Spot said. 'We'll carry out the examination.'

Some time later Spot said: 'Very disappointing. Nothing to go on whatsoever.' He thought for a moment. 'Of course,' he said slowly, 'there's no reason why you shouldn't say that the pain is too much to bear, anyway, and you think you need being circumcised.'

'Don't talk such rot,' Cyril said. He looked flushed and embarrassed, and was obviously wishing that the subject had never been brought up.

'Think of it,' Spot said, 'you'd be the first man to bludge your way off a working party with that.'

'I don't think it would work,' I said. 'For one thing, I don't think that the Germans would think there was much point in doing the operation, not in Cyril's circumstances.'

'Rubbish!' Spot said. 'The man is in great pain—at least he will be by the time he reaches the M.O.' He looked at Cyril. 'You are going to have a bash, aren't you?'

'I don't know,' Cyril said doubtfully. 'Even if I got away with it, it seems rather a heavy price to pay.'

'I don't know what you're griping about,' Spot said in exasperation. 'People are cutting off their fingers, breaking their arms, and doing God knows what to get out of the mines. You've got the chance of getting out with a perfectly simple little operation. What's the matter with you?'

Cyril was silent for a while. 'All right,' he said finally. 'I'll have a go.'

We all personally escorted Cyril over to the sick-bay, in

case he should change his mind. I don't think any of us really thought he would get away with it, but it made a welcome diversion for the Sunday morning.

But we were wrong. Cyril did get away with it. Perhaps the doctor thought that anyone who had the nerve to think up a scheme like that deserved to get out of the mines, anyway. The M.O. made an application to the Stalag for them to take Cyril, and a few weeks later he left.

A prisoner returning from the Stalag after a period in the *Lazarette* there informed us that the patient was doing well.

Determined not to be outdone by Cyril, I began seeking for a way in which I could get myself back to the Stalag. As Spot seemed to be temporarily lacking in inspiration, I mulled over most of the tried and tested ideas, but as even the idea of executing any of them gave me the shudders, I rejected them. Finally, I fell back on the good old foot-breaking idea, a simple and not too bloody process that merely involved getting someone to drop a large pit log on your foot. To help me carry out this operation, I called on Arthur for assistance.

We were on haulage in the pit at the time, transporting the logs from the pit-heads to the different sections. When we were in a quiet part of the mine, I pulled one of the logs and let it fall with a sickening crash to the ground.

'There,' I said to Arthur, 'now pick it up and drop it on my foot. Try to break it.'

Arthur looked at me for a moment and then shrugged his shoulders. With some difficulty he lifted the log from the ground and, staggering under the weight of it, he said breathlessly: 'Now, are you quite sure...?'

I extended my foot and closed one eye. 'Get on with it,' I said. 'Drop it!'

As Arthur dropped it, I quickly withdrew my foot.

'We'll try again,' I said.

We tried again, and once again I withdrew my foot just

in time. This happened several times, and then I gave up.

'I don't know how they do it,' I said, wiping the perspiration off my face. 'I'll have to think of something else.'

Back in the barrack-room that evening, I gave some more thought to the matter. It was clear to me now that I was not really prepared to do anything drastic to get out of the mine. I should have to be content with a few days off instead. Perhaps after that I might feel better equipped to face another long spell down the pit. What I needed was some nice, not too painful, not too dangerous injury that would keep me rested up for a while without too much discomfort. Then I remembered that I had a faint bruise on my chest, which I had got through being hit by a runaway wagon. I opened my shirt and looked at it thoughtfully. It was at that moment that Tiger came into the room.

'Tiger,' I said, 'how would you like to give me a real good wallop?'

Tiger stared at me and then scowled. 'Are you trying to be funny?'

'No,' I said. 'Just wanting to get out of the mine for a few days. I'm sick of it.' I showed him the bruise. 'Now if you could give me a good hard punch on that, it might bring up something worth taking over to the quack.'

Tiger said he would be only too pleased to oblige. I could see a nasty gleam in his eye as we prepared for the operation. Standing up, I bared my chest. Tiger took sights on the bruise with one fist, while he gently moved my head sideways with his free hand.

'Just shut your eyes,' Tiger said softly.

I closed my eyes, and as I did so Tiger's fist exploded against my chest. I remember sailing through the air and crashing against the cupboard, and after that, nothing.

When I came to among the splintered ruins of the cupboard, Tiger was hovering solicitously over me.

'You've got a real lovely bruise there,' he said. 'A real beauty.' He looked at it with a craftsman's pride.

THE ART OF GOING SICK

Staggering to my feet, I reeled over to the sick-bay and was promptly admitted. Tiger came over to see me several times, and took an almost ghoulish delight in examining the progress of the bruise, as it turned from a deep purple to a bright yellow.

CHAPTER EIGHT

Women!

It had always rather saddened Arthur and me that we had never derived any particular profit from our struggles with the German language. We had acquired the ability to pick the bones out of a German newspaper, and occasionally some foreman had given us a cushy job, merely so that we would have time to listen to a lengthy discourse on how and why England was going to lose the war. But that was the sole sum of our achievements. The coveted jobs on 'Staff' had never materialized, and as far as Arthur and I could see never would.

It therefore came as a complete surprise when the English Sergeant in charge told us that there were staff jobs for us at a new camp opening up less than a mile away. On the day the camp opened, we packed our few possessions, said our good-byes to envious friends, and then departed in the custody of two guards, rejoicing in our good fortune.

As soon as we saw the new camp, our rejoicings abruptly ceased. The camp that we had left behind us had had painted barracks, flower-beds, gravelled paths, and a general air of friendliness about it that had made one occasionally forget the barbed wire and the sentry posts. The new camp was a squalid abomination that looked as if it had been built on a dumping ground for all the local rubbish. Three large, ramshackle barracks looked out on an open patch of ground littered with rubble, old tins, sodden newspapers, and various other unidentifiable items of refuse that looked as if a close inspection might bring on a severe attack of vomiting. There were no houses around the camp, only more wasteland, pitted with holes and strewn with twisted lumps

of rusty iron. Apart from a single prisoner walking across
the compound, the camp was deserted.

The wooden gates of the camp swung open to admit us.
The prisoner walking across the compound changed his
course and came towards us. He looked dirty and unshaven,
and also very bad tempered. Rather unwisely, I thought,
Arthur stopped him.

'Where's the Sergeant?'

'How the hell should I know?' The prisoner scowled at
us. 'Anyway, what do you want him for?'

'We've come to join the staff,' I said.

The prisoner looked at us stonily. 'So you're two more of
the bastards. Come to sit around on your backsides and give
orders while we poor sods tear out our guts down the mine.'

Rather quickly Arthur and I moved on.

'Maybe it's not going to be such fun being on staff, after
all,' I said.

'What did you expect?' Arthur said. 'Nobody is going to
like us from now on.'

Arthur was right, of course. Staff were automatically considered to be guilty of fiddling rations, stealing Red Cross
parcels, and sucking up to the Germans. Although I knew
that the real reason for their unpopularity was more a matter of plain jealousy than anything else, I still found it rather
disturbing to realize that I was now one of the unloved.

'I suppose we'd better start searching for the Sergeant in
the barracks,' I said.

As I spoke, an English Sergeant came out of one of the
barracks, accompanied by an Unteroffizier. Ever since we
had left the old camp, I had been wondering if we were
going to be condemned to live with some time-serving old
sweat with nothing on his mind but his years of service and
the desire to impose a lot of army bull on us. The Sergeant,
I noted with relief, was a young man, about the same age
as ourselves.

'Thank Christ, you two have arrived,' the Sergeant said,

as he came up to us. 'Which of you is supposed to be the interpreter?'

'Arthur's the interpreter,' I said, 'and I'm your new clerk, general odd-bod man and assistant interpreter.'

'Glad to meet you, boys,' the Sergeant said. 'The name's Harry. No need for army formalities here.' He pointed a finger at the Unteroffizier who had now arrived beside him. 'This is the Kommandant. He wants the men on parade for work tomorrow morning, but you can tell him from me that no man is leaving this camp until this muck-heap has been cleaned up.'

The Unteroffizier, a grizzled, middle-aged man with steel-rimmed spectacles, listened attentively while Arthur translated.

'Coal for the German Reich is more important than cleaning the camp,' the Kommandant said portentously after Arthur had finished. 'The men can do that in their spare time. You will please tell the Sergeant that if he does not get the men on parade tomorrow morning, my guards will come into the camp with bayonets.'

It all sounded sadly familiar. Arthur passed on the Kommandant's remarks, and we both waited anxiously for Harry's next move.

'Well,' Harry said briskly, 'sort it out, boys.'

'How?' Arthur asked blankly.

'That's what you're here for, isn't it?' Harry said. 'To sort out things like this. Both of you. Let's see you earn your keep.'

'Oh,' I said. The mine seemed almost a desirable place to be in at that moment. 'Over to you,' I said, nudging Arthur in the ribs. 'You're the official interpreter here.'

I stood back and waited for the inevitable explosion from the Kommandant. But Arthur's years of experience in dealing with difficult foremen had not been spent in vain. Arthur pointed out to the Kommandant that it would perhaps be wiser if he started off on the right foot by showing the men that they had an understanding Kommandant who had their interests at heart. The men would appreciate it and respond by working harder. Getting into his stride, Arthur spoke of how the British could not live under the dirty conditions which existed in the camp at the moment. The Kommandant, as a member of a race noted for its cleanliness, must understand how they felt.

When Arthur had finished, the Kommandant looked at him for a long time in silence. 'Tomorrow to clean the camp,' he said finally, 'and then the men go out to work.' Saluting gravely, he walked away.

'Well, I suppose that's something,' Harry said, as we all watched the Kommandant heading for the German barrack that was just outside the main gate. 'Now let's go over to our room and have a general natter about things.'

'Where is everyone?' I asked, as we strolled across the yard.

'Gone to bed so that they won't have to look at the camp,' Harry said. 'No one is very happy about it.'

'I can't say I blame them,' I said. 'I don't think I am either.'

The room that had been set aside for the staff cheered me up considerably. It was about twice the size of the room I had shared with seven other men at the previous camp, and instead of bunks there were iron beds with spring mattresses on them.

'Very nice,' I said, looking around the room. 'We should be very comfortable here.'

'Never mind that,' Harry said irritably, 'let's get down to discussing what we can do to get this camp running the way we want it to.'

'Here we go,' I murmured. 'Red Cross goodies for the guards.'

'I think we can forget about the guards for the time being,' Harry said. 'But you've got the general idea. Let's concentrate on the Kommandant. Unless we get him sewn up quickly, we're going to have real trouble. You'd better get him over now, and we'll see what can be done with him. No sense in wasting time.'

'Shouldn't we go over to him?' I suggested.

'Certainly not,' Harry said. 'The only way to deal with a German is to show him who is boss right away. Now get over there and tell him I want to see him. Use any excuse you like, but get him over here.'

So I went over to the Kommandant's office and told him that the English Sergeant wanted to see him in strict privacy on a most serious matter concerning the welfare of the camp. The Kommandant came immediately, looking genuinely alarmed. When we arrived at the staff room, Harry was waiting for us, an open Red Cross parcel on the table in front of him.

'You'd better leave us,' Harry told me; 'too many of us around might make him uneasy.'

I left the Kommandant to the tender mercies of Harry and Arthur. I felt quite sorry for him.

A few minutes later the Kommandant came out of the staff room, tight-lipped and angry-looking. As I went back, Harry was swearing softly.

'Do you know what he said?' Harry said angrily. 'He said that he had no need to take food from prisoners. The German Reich knows how to look after its soldiers.'

'A lie,' I said, 'but very patriotic. I must say it makes a change to find an honest Kommandant.'

'Don't be a damn fool,' Harry said rudely. 'We'll just have to find a way to get rid of him, that's all.'

Harry's opportunity to get rid of the Kommandant came soon afterwards, when a German officer visited the camp to find out if we had any complaints. Harry immediately told him that the Kommandant had bred a great feeling of discontent in the camp by imposing a lot of unnecessary restrictions that were bound to lead to a general strike among the men. The Kommandant, who had only done his duty, left within the week.

The new Kommandant who took over was much more to

our liking. Unteroffizier Lober came from Munich, and according to him had held a post of some responsibility in the city. If the post had anything to do with public funds, the people of Munich had my sympathy, for Lober was probably the most venal Kommandant in the whole of Germany.

Unteroffizier Lober was prepared to agree to anything for a tin of sardines or a few cigarettes, as long as it did not entail any personal risk to himself. As it happened, our immediate demands were not exacting: As high a daily sick roster as could be allowed without exciting the suspicion of the mine owners; an hour's walk once a day in the company of a guard for the three of us, whenever we wanted it (a privilege accorded to most of the higher orders of staff, anyway), and complete freedom for the men to bring in whatever food they had managed to buy on the black market. Puffing contentedly at an English cigarette, Unteroffizier Lober was most happy to agree.

Now that the camp had been cleaned up and was functioning properly, it was really no worse than any other working party in the district. Taking into consideration that we had a Kommandant who was prepared to be most cooperative as long as his cupboard remained stocked with Red Cross tins and his case full of English cigarettes, it was probably better than most.

For me, at least, it was just about the best I could expect as a prisoner. The work was certainly not arduous; a roll-call at five-thirty in the morning, before nipping sharply back to bed; some interpreting whenever Arthur wasn't around; a couple of hours' clerical duty in the German *Schreibstube*, and finally, at the end of the day, a quiet walk around the barracks accompanying a guard on his rounds before the lights went out. The rest of the time was spent in reading, cooking, and writing up the journal I had been working on since 1941. Sometimes I went for a walk in the company of a guard, but not as often as I might have done. The Polish winters are severe and not easy to ignore, and the bitter winds that whistled across the fields outside the camp were certainly no inducement for me to leave the fire that was kept going day and night in the staff room.

A young Scots M.O. arrived from Stalag VIIIB and took up residence in the staff room with us, and at first we bitterly resented the intrusion of an officer into our cosy set-up. But Mac, the M.O., was a kind and gentle soul, ill-equipped to deal with the prisoners who crowded into the sick-bay every day, savagely determined to get on the sick list, and before long we were adopting an almost protective attitude towards him. Mac hated to call any man a liar, and although it pained him deeply to betray his professional pride by pretending to be taken in by the lies that were told him, he would mark down the most blatant case of malingering as being unfit for work rather than have any unpleasantness in the sick-bay. In the end the sick lists became so long that even Lober had to protest. After that, Harry went through every sick list, striking off half the names that Mac had put on it.

Mac thoroughly deplored the methods we used for making life generally easier for the camp, but was too weak to do anything about it. When the camp eventually became so corrupt as to need an injection of sharp discipline to put it on its feet again, Mac evaded his responsibilities as an officer by withdrawing from camp life completely, and after that the camp saw him only on the two sick parades he held each day.

Mac was weak, but still rather a lovable man in many ways, and the only thing I ever had again him was his ability to scrounge cigarettes off me. He did it superbly, taking them from me as if our respective natural functions in life were for me to give and him to receive. In the end I took to smoking a pipe.

Our troubles really started from the moment some of the prisoners began asking the guards if it was possible for them to be taken out for walks after working hours. The guards, banding together into a sort of guards' union, said that for five cigarettes a day they would be most pleased to take any prisoner for a walk, but naturally Lober's consent had to be obtained. Lober was only too willing to give his consent— providing that he also received five cigarettes from each man going out for a walk.

The men who went on those walks found them most pleasant, even allowing for the weather, but a little unsettling. There were so many young and attractive girls in the streets; girls who smiled provocatively and looked as if they would be very willing to grant favours if given the opportunity. With the sort of guards we had, the next step was almost inevitable.

The guards' union informed the prisoners that for cigarettes, many more cigarettes, they would be prepared to allow any prisoner to strike up an acquaintance with some girl and make a date with her for an evening meeting at some deserted spot outside the village. As Lober had already shown that he was not the sort of man to encourage private enterprise without wanting a substantial share of the profits for himself, the guards omitted to inform him of the improvement they had made on the original scheme.

The scheme was so successful that it was not long before the camp was full of moon-struck men, waiting irritably until their turn came around to go out for another walk and another meeting with the newly found girl friend. As the guards had a long list of clients, they often had to wait weeks before their turn came around. None of it improved the general disposition of the camp.

But the situation did not really get out of hand until after the opening night of the *Gefangener's* brothel. This was an inspired idea on the part of one of the guards, who made a deal with one of the local prostitutes, and then smuggled her into the camp bath-house under cover of darkness. After this had been safely accomplished, he came into our room and proudly announced that the brothel was now open to anyone who cared to patronize it. The bath-house was outside the compound, and twenty cigarettes was the exit fee. The guard was a little apologetic that he had to charge so much, but operational costs had been high. There had not only been the guard on the gate to fix, but also the guard on the watch-tower near the gate. The lady, now waiting expectantly in the darkness of the bath-house, would be quite content if she received either a pair of woollen socks or a bar of chocolate from each man she entertained.

Although neither Harry, Arthur, nor I were prepared to give the venture our active support, we willingly passed the news around. From the way the gates kept opening and closing for the rest of the evening, we gathered that the guard had no shortage of clients.

The camp brothel was a short-lived affair and lasted only the one night. Early next morning the guard who had organized it came storming into our room.

'The English are swine,' he shouted. 'Men without honour. They do not deserve to be treated with kindness. You do things for them and then they betray you.'

'What's the matter?' Arthur asked quietly.

The guard fumbled in his pocket and pulled out one of the thin bars of chocolate which were in all the Canadian Red Cross parcels we had been receiving lately, and also a pair of army woollen socks.

'Look at them,' the guard shouted, throwing the chocolate and socks on the table. 'Look at them, and see how the honourable English behave.'

When we examined them we found that the chocolate wrapping contained a piece of slate and that the socks were full of holes.

'Every one was the same,' the guard said bitterly. 'That poor woman didn't know she was being swindled. How could she, working in the dark, and with so many to deal with?' The thought of it all seemed to overcome him for a moment, and he lapsed into silence.

Harry chuckled softly. 'What a shower!' he said, grinning. 'They must have got together and rummaged out some of that slate that's been lying at the barracks since the huts were first built. They don't miss a trick, do they?'

'A silly thing to do, though,' Arthur said. 'Now they've spoilt it for themselves. We could have been the only prisoner-of-war camp in Germany with its own brothel.'

The guard suddenly came to life. 'The lady, of course, must be compensated.' He looked at us hopefully.

'Get out,' Arthur said evenly, 'unless you want me to tell Lober all about this—and about what happens on all those walks you take the prisoners on.'

The guard left quickly. Like the rest of the guards, he feared Lober second only to being sent to the Russian Front.

'Well,' Harry said, once the guard had gone, 'as far as I can see, we're booked for some difficult times. You mark my words, before long this camp is going to be turned into a proper madhouse, and before it's all finished we're going to be lucky if we're not all out of this room and down the mine ourselves.'

But the problem of how to deal with the sexual urges of the camp was taken out of our hands, for a while at least, by the evening walks being brought to an abrupt halt in a way that none of us on the staff had quite anticipated.

On the night of the disaster that was to make a lot of love-sick prisoners very unhappy, Harry and I were taking a walk around the compound before turning in. It was a clear night, and for a moment we both stopped to look up at the stars shining like hard diamonds in the black sky above us. Faintly we could hear the sound of singing voices approaching the camp.

'Some of the guards coming home drunk,' Harry said casually. 'Lober will have something to say about that.'

We continued on our stroll until we were standing by the gates. The singing was louder now, but we did not really take much notice of it. It was not the first time that guards had come back to the barracks drunk. And then, suddenly, Harry clutched my arm.

'Listen,' Harry said.

I listened. There were two voices singing, and quite distinctly I could hear one of them giving an off-key rendering of 'Oh, my darling Clementine.'

The guard in the watch-tower began to make frantic signals to the guard on the gate, and then, out of the darkness came two figures; the figures of a German guard and a British prisoner locked in an affectionate embrace, and bawling lustily. With a sort of fascinated horror I watched their staggering progress towards the gates of the camp.

'Oh, my God!' Harry said. 'Even Lober won't stand for this sort of thing.'

Reaching the gates, the two drunks came to a halt and finished off their different choruses in a hideous cacophony of sound that must have been heard in Piaski.

'*Ruhe!*' hissed the guard on the gate. '*Ruhe!*'

He looked quickly towards the German barracks, some yards away, and then fumbled for his keys. But that last exuberant outburst of song had destroyed any chance he might have had of smuggling the prisoner back into the camp. The door of the German barracks flew open with a crash, and Lober appeared on the steps.

'What goes?' he shouted.

Then he saw the two figures locked in each other's arms.

I had never seen Lober move so fast as he did then. Before the guard had even finished opening the gate to let us out, Lober was with us.

'Drunk,' Lober was saying as we joined him. 'Both drunk.' He looked as if he were about to faint.

The two drunks had now disengaged themselves, and were looking at Lober with owlish gravity. Both Harry and I knew that the situation needed being brought to a speedy close before the two of them began babbling about some of the other things that had probably been going on that night. Taking our drunk by each arm, we began to move towards the gate.

'We will look after him,' I said to Lober. 'It is nothing to worry about.'

Lober bounded forward beside us. 'Fool!' he shouted. 'Don't you realize that if these two swine have been seen by a German, the matter is almost bound to be reported. In that case, the Gestapo will be here in the morning, and that will be the end of me.'

Harry and I kept going, dragging the drunk along between us. 'That's your worry,' I said over my shoulder to Lober. 'Yours and the guard's. Not ours. The Englishman can't be blamed for this.'

'The Englishman goes into the bunker tomorrow,' Lober thundered behind us. 'And from tomorrow there will also be some changes in this camp.'

'And that, if I'm not much mistaken,' Harry said grimly as the gates closed behind us, 'is the end of the walks, among other things.'

Harry was quite right. Although there was no visit from the Gestapo, Lober had received a fright, and he had no intention of laying himself open to any more like it. Cigarettes or no cigarettes, walks were now definitely out. In the first stages of his panic, Lober also threatened to stop food coming into the camp and to cut out the sick list. When we coldly pointed out to him that this would absolve us from the need to give him anything from the Red Cross parcels, Lober had second thoughts about the matter. But nothing could make him change his mind about the walks.

But neither the guards nor the prisoners had any intention of leaving it at that. The guards had got used to smoking heavily, and the prisoners had got used to freedom and some of the things that went with it, and neither intended to give up what they had gained without a struggle.

The guards started the ball rolling by quietly making a small hole in the barbed wire near one of the watch-towers. The idea was that any prisoner wanting to go through the wire had to contact the first available guard and give him the exit fee, which would be handed over to the guard on duty in the watch-tower on the particular night the prisoner intended to get out. The guard on duty would then let him slip through the wire and come back again without putting a bullet in his back.

This was a scheme fraught with the most frightful dangers. There was the possibility that the cigarettes might not be passed on, or that the guards' shift might be changed at the last moment, both contingencies that would mean someone getting shot. Added to these was the risk that some guard with a perverted sense of humour would shoot, anyway. The scheme therefore did not attract many, and the few foolhardy ones who did go through the wire went through it only once. They said that the strain of going through the wire under the watchful eye of a guard behind a machine-gun was a little too much to endure, even for a woman.

The guards now had to think of something else, and in the end they picked on Emmy, Lober's washerwoman. Nothing was sacred to the guards.

Emmy was a Pole in her late thirties, a blonde, plump woman with a permanently vague look in her eyes. Ever since Lober had taken over the camp, she had been coming every Saturday night to the German barracks to collect his dirty washing. The *Schreibstube* was next to Lober's room, and as Saturday evening was when I had to type out the work lists for the following week, I had always been present at the little performance, which for a long time had heralded Emmy's arrival. Emmy would come down the passage, knock softly at Lober's door, and then smile gently at me through the glass door of the office. Lober would then come to the door, looking brisk and business-like.

'Ah! Emmy! The washing isn't ready yet, so you had better come in and help me pack it.' Lober would say this loudly for my benefit, and then the door would close behind them.

Lober packing washing with Emmy was a noisy business, involving creaking springs, giggles from Emmy, and some stifled sheep-like braying from Lober. After it was all over, Emmy would emerge from Lober's room and depart placidly down the passage, lugging a great bag of washing over her shoulder.

Recently, however, there had been a change in the proceedings. Lober now left his dirty washing in the passage for Emmy to collect. He, it seemed, no longer enjoyed packing up the washing with Emmy.

The guards' idea was that as Lober was no longer interested in Emmy, he should be relieved of the embarrassment of seeing her around. If Lober would agree to it, the prisoners could take turns in carrying Lober's washing down to her house. Emmy, the guards assured us, was sex mad. Any visitors would be made most welcome. Unsuspectingly, Lober agreed to the suggestion, and at once Operation Emmy was put into action.

The first two volunteers came back with some interesting reports, and a roster was put into being at once. For months afterwards, sharp on the stroke of four o'clock on every Saturday afternoon, two prisoners bounced expectantly down Emmy's garden path, carrying Lober's washing between them. The guard remained in the street, or casually inspected Emmy's flower-beds, until they came out again. Emmy was, I think, a little dazed to find herself suddenly the belle of the camp.

But the Emmy set-up did not solve the problems of those who had got themselves emotionally involved before the evening walks had been stopped. The guards listened to their suggestions with sympathetic consideration, for Emmy brought in only very small pickings, and if any practical scheme could be put forward to improve the situation, they were only too willing to listen. But the schemes suggested to them were wild and dangerous, and very firmly the guards rejected them. In desperation, the guards finally decided that a chosen few, men who could be trusted not to betray them, would be let out once a week to make their way to wherever they wanted to go. If they were caught, they were to pretend they had escaped, and would have to take the consequences without dragging the guards into it.

Walking through the streets of Piaski without a guard was dangerous, for policemen roamed through the village from dusk till dawn. Fortunately for everyone concerned, the few prisoners that were let out under a solemn pledge not to betray the guard if they were caught, always returned to the camp without having been seen. One prisoner partially solved the problem by first visiting a Polish mining friend who lived near the camp, and after borrowing the wife's clothes, quite openly went the rest of the way in the guise of a woman. He swore that on one occasion a Gestapo man had tried to pick him up, but personally I never really believed the story.

Arthur and I lived in perpetual fear of the day when Lober would find out about the high jinks going on in the camp. When that day came, there would be some sweeping changes in the staff, and quite clearly, Arthur and I could see ourselves being booted back down the mine.

But everything continued to go very smoothly, and the only real trouble was caused by a certain rugged Scotsman who kept persisting in the belief that he was quite capable of getting out of the camp without any help from the guards. His first abortive attempt had been to start digging a tunnel through the floor of his room. Lober had discovered it by accident, and there had been a very unpleasant scene. A tin of cigarettes had finally ended the matter, but for a long time afterwards Lober kept disturbing the barracks to inspect the state of the floor-boards.

Attempt number two was another dismal failure. Occasionally, some of the prisoners were allowed to go and work in a nearby bakery in their spare time. The work was not hard, and it always meant the present of a loaf of bread for every man as he left. Undaunted by the failure of the tunnel, our Scotsman got on to the bakery party, helped himself to one of the baker's overalls, and was on his way out of the back door when the guard caught him. That was the end of the bakery detail.

Attempt number three was a success, even if it did leave

the rest of the camp in no mood to hand out congratulations. Every morning a Pole from the bakery came into the camp pushing a small, closed-in hand-cart filled with the camp bread. The Scot knew that the bread cart was never inspected when it went out of the camp, and one day the Pole arrived at the cookhouse to find a British prisoner waiting for him with a profitable and fairly safe proposition. A deal was done on the spot, and the Scot went out in the bread cart.

It was not until just before the evening roll-call that one of his friends deigned to tell Harry that he would be one man short for the parade. When Harry heard what had happened, he hit the roof.

'They don't care, do they?' Harry said savagely. 'They don't care if they do get put in the bunker as long as they've had a chance to see their women. And they don't care what happens to anyone else, either.'

'It's not as bad as all that, Harry,' I said. 'He knows that we can cover up for him for one night. His pals say he's coming back in the bread cart tomorrow.'

'Maybe you've forgotten,' Harry said acidly, 'but that cart is supposed to contain the camp's bread when it comes in here, not some skirt-mad Scotsman. With him in it, there won't be room for any bread.'

The loss of a day's bread ration for the entire camp was bad enough. When something went wrong on the evening roll-call and we were unable to cover up for the missing Scot, we were really in trouble.

Lober came storming into the staff room, convinced that the escape had received our backing. He was naturally thinking of the escape in terms of someone having got out of the camp for the soldierly reason of trying to get back to his own country. In a case like that the escapee would most certainly first have consulted the British Officer and Sergeant in charge before making his attempt, and as Lober knew this, we had no success whatsoever in our attempts to persuade him that we had had no hand in the affair. When he left us, he was still speaking of *Strafe Lagers* and the salt-mines.

The next morning the bread cart arrived in the camp as usual, and when the Scotsman clambered out of it behind the shelter of the cookhouse, he found Harry waiting there to whisk him off to Lober's office. The story was that the prisoner had fallen asleep in one of the latrines and had been missed by the guards who had not seen him in the darkness. It was a pretty thin story, but the presence of the prisoner seemed to back it up, and Lober allowed the two of them to return to the camp without further questioning.

A little later Lober paid us a visit in the staff room. He had spoken to the guard who had searched the latrines, and he had assured Lober that he had examined them most carefully. Since then Lober had been doing some thinking. It was possible that the prisoner had escaped and then come back into the camp. If that was so, he had not got out of the camp to make an escape, but for some other reason. A woman, perhaps? While Lober watched us closely from beneath raised eyebrows, we made good-humoured signs of disbelief, and generally did our best to ridicule the idea of prisoners having girl friends. Anyway, said Lober, he was going out to make a few enquiries. He hoped for the sake of everyone that they would come to nothing.

Lober had actually carried his thinking beyond what he had told us. For one thing, he had remembered the guards' rather over-eager desire to protect him from Emmy, and so, when he went out later that day to pursue his enquiries, Emmy's house was the first stop. He had no need to go any farther.

Lober returned to the camp and began grilling his guards in his office. Afterwards he came over to see us. From the noise that had been coming from Lober's room when he had been interviewing his guards, we knew that all was not well, and, in anticipation of trouble, Harry had thoughtfully placed a Red Cross parcel on the table. When Lober arrived, he was surprisingly quiet but very bitter about it all.

'The guards have confessed to everything,' Lober said. 'I told them that if they did not do so, I would have them all transferred to the Eastern Front.' His gaze fell on the Red Cross box, and then resolutely he turned away from it. 'I do not mind making life easier for the prisoners, but not at the risk of losing my head,' Lober continued. 'You have all betrayed my trust in you, even my own guards. Now you shall see that I can be a bad Kommandant just as easily as I was a good Kommandant. From now on it is all going to be very different.'

Lober went on to tell us how it was going to be different. No more contraband allowed into the camp; no more football in the compound; no more sick lists; no more hob-nobbing with the guards. No more privileges of any sort. As for the staff, it would depend on how we behaved in the future. Lober's gaze fell briefly on the Red Cross parcel again.

There was no doubt that Lober's nerves were very badly frayed by the knowledge of how his guards had betrayed him. The next day Lober came across his pet goat nibbling at his prize flower-bed, and shot it on sight. I suppose he felt that he was no longer able to trust anyone, not even the goat.

CHAPTER NINE

The Gestapo versus The Rest

UNTEROFFIZIER LOBER was a crook, but not basically a hard man, and after a while he lifted some of the restrictions he had imposed upon us, including the embargo on contraband.

But no sooner had we weathered our troubles with Lober than we were presented with another set of problems. Rather belatedly, the Gestapo had come to the conclusion that the mixing of Poles with British prisoners had some aspects about it that might prove dangerous as far as the Germans were concerned. The Poles, always a proud and violent race, had shown that they were not content to be submissive in defeat, and therefore there was the possibility that they might smuggle weapons into the camps, incite the prisoners to mutiny, or at the very least help them to get a wireless into camp.

The Gestapo's fears were not entirely unjustified. When I had been on the other working party, the local Resistance had sent us a message through an intermediary in the mine. If we were agreeable, they would storm the camp, release us, and give us arms so that we could fight side by side with them. Thoroughly alarmed at the prospect of getting involved in this hare-brained scheme, we had politely but very quickly declined. On behalf of the camp, however, the English Sergeant in charge had gladly accepted the offer of a wireless that had been delivered down the mine and from there smuggled into the camp in sections.

Although we certainly had no arms in the camp, the Gestapo raids worried us. There was the matter of contraband, which was strictly forbidden, and if found would lead to trouble for the Poles. Fortunately the Gestapo always made the mistake of telephoning the camp Kommandant to let him know they were on the way. A phone call like this was enough to throw any Kommandant into a state of panic. He knew that if anything was found in his camp, even contraband food, he would be on the mat for inefficiency, and quite likely sent to the Russian Front on account of it. His natural instinct, therefore, was to throw in his lot with the prisoners for a few hours, in a mutual conspiracy to conceal anything that might upset the Gestapo.

We saw how this worked when the Gestapo paid us their first visit. Lober was away on leave, presumably recuperating from the strain of looking after us, and the relief Kommandant in charge was a sour-faced individual who spoke English and whom none of us liked. On the morning of the search, he came bustling into our room while we were having breakfast. He looked at the Red Cross parcel and the tins on the table.

'The Gestapo are on their way, and will be with us within the hour.'

Harry deliberately picked up the pound tin of Canadian butter and began to smear butter thickly on his bread. The Kommandant watched him with positive loathing.

'What are we supposed to have done now?' Harry asked him finally.

'It's a search for contraband,' the Kommandant said heavily. 'How much of it is there in the camp?'

We looked at him indignantly.

'Listen,' the Kommandant said wearily. 'I know this camp is full of it. Food bought from the Poles down the mine and smuggled into the camp. Even a wireless, perhaps.' He shuddered at the thought.

'In that case,' Harry said cheerfully, 'the Gestapo will soon find it.'

A stricken look came over the Kommandant's face. He hesitated and then said suddenly: 'I will strike a bargain with you. If all your men pass over their contraband to me, I will put it away in my cupboards. The Gestapo will not search our barracks, and I know that I can trust my men. When the Gestapo have gone, I promise I will hand it all back again.'

Harry looked at me. 'Can we trust him?'

'If he takes it, the worst that can happen is that we'll lose the lot,' I said. 'If the Gestapo find it, half of this camp will land up in a *Strafe Lager*.'

'All right,' Harry said, turning to the Kommandant. 'We'll have the stuff over to your barracks within the next quarter of an hour.'

The Kommandant wiped his brow. 'Good. But let us do this quickly. I have no desire to go to the Russian Front.'

After he had gone, we began to rush around the barracks. Although we pretended to be casual about the whole matter to the Kommandant, we knew that the situation was quite serious. There was a great deal of cursing from each room as we went into them one by one, but eventually a steady stream of men carrying little brown boxes began to trickle out of the barracks and through the open gates, where the perspiring Kommandant stood by his window, ready to take the boxes from the men as they passed.

A few minutes after all the contraband had been stowed away in the Kommandant's cupboards and the gates shut on us again, two cars arrived outside the camp. Several men, wearing those heavy leather macks that were the hall-mark of the Gestapo, stepped out. Even with their macks and their slouch hats they looked more like prosperous business-men than members of the dreaded Gestapo.

The Gestapo were obviously disappointed when the search revealed nothing. Afterwards, a short conversation was held outside the camp, during which there was much finger-wagging at the Kommandant, who kept bobbing his head up and down in violent agreement. As soon as they were gone the gates opened again, and the Kommandant took his place at the window, ready to deal with the long line of waiting men who had come to reclaim their property.

I was never able to reconcile the cold politeness of the

Gestapo during the searches with their inhuman treatment of political prisoners. It was, I think, merely another manifestation of the German official's attitude, which was always based on an established conception of how each alien stood in the German world order of things. Every nation was mentally categorized under some tired propaganda cliché. The British were soldiers, with a military tradition that should be respected, but had to be shown who were the masters; the French, an effete race but useful; the Italians, a joke; the Poles, little better than the Jews; the Russians, wild beasts not worthy of consideration as human beings. On a lesser scale, they had the same attitude to their own people. Heavy workers were useful members of the Third Reich as long as they could work twelve to sixteen hours a day, and therefore deserved the extra rations that kept them going. If you were weak, not even good enough for cannon fodder, you could subsist on the bare rations and perhaps die of tuberculosis, and thereby save the food for those who really earned it.

We were not so lucky with the Gestapo's next visit to the camp. This time they signalled their impending arrival by phoning through to the Kommandant the night before they were due to arrive. This would have been fine if the relief Kommandant had still been there. Unfortunately, he wasn't. In his place was a much younger man, who on his arrival had immediately instituted a regular search of the prisoners as they returned from the mines. This had caused inconvenience, but had not been insurmountable. It just meant that goods cost us more, as now we had to bribe the guards to allow the contraband to pass into the camp.

The night the Gestapo phoned through, I was summoned to the Kommandant's office.

'The Gestapo are coming tomorrow,' he said coldly. 'I therefore intend to search each barrack myself to make sure that nothing has slipped past the guards.'

All went well until we entered one of the rooms in the

second barrack. As we stepped into it, everyone began to talk at the top of their voices.

'It's a search,' I shouted above the din. 'The Kommandant wants to make sure there's nothing here that will upset the Gestapo, who are coming into the camp tomorrow.'

Someone muttered something very rude from his bunk, and the next moment the room was in an uproar again. Although the Kommandant could not speak English, he obviously recognized the Anglo-Saxon word that kept recurring with monotonous regularity.

'What are they saying?' he asked suspiciously.

'They are assuring you that they have no forbidden goods in the room,' I told him.

As I spoke, the room suddenly took on an appearance of frenzied activity. One man was busily engaged in hammering his bed-boards together, while another sat perched on the edge of his bunk playing a mouth organ with more enthusiasm than ability. A small group was gathered around the fire, arguing loudly among themselves about who was to have the fire next to do the cooking. No one took any notice of the Kommandant. The Kommandant looked uncertainly around the room.

'Do they give their word as Englishmen that there is nothing in this room?'

Everyone paused just long enough to let off a stream of blistering abuse.

'Of course,' I said icily.

The Kommandant seemed satisfied. As he began to walk out of the room, he idly opened one of the cupboards. A sudden hush fell over the room. The next moment a large goose stepped out of the cupboard and waddled swiftly into the middle of the room.

The Kommandant looked down at the goose. The goose hesitated for a moment, then, hissing loudly, made a sudden dart for the Kommandant. The Kommandant began to retreat towards the door.

'Tell them to take that bird to the German barracks,' he

bawled from the doorway. He looked down at the goose, whose head was weaving ominously in his direction. 'If it isn't there within fifteen minutes, the whole room goes in the bunker for a week.'

The next moment he was gone. Soon afterwards we heard a resounding crash next door, followed by a series of loud thuds. After I had passed the Kommandant's message on to the stricken room, I reluctantly went to join the Kommandant next door. In the short space of time he had been there, the Kommandant had reduced it to a state of chaos. Tins, bedding, Red Cross boxes, cooking utensils, books, and other articles littered the room. Among it all stood the Kommandant, now grimly occupied in pushing a cupboard to the floor. I never did find a German with a sense of humour.

The Kommandant's methods were crude but effective. By the time he had finished, the whole camp was in a shambles, and the Kommandant in possession of enough dead poultry, eggs, tomatoes, and other delicacies to keep the whole of the German barracks going for months.

Although the Gestapo search went off quietly the next day, the incident of the goose had its repercussions on the camp for some time. Such concessions as Sunday football were stopped, Red Cross parcels were held back so that we no longer received them weekly, and, worst of all, the searches at the gate became so rigid that it was almost impossible to smuggle food into the camp. Fortunately, Lober came back from leave at long last, and all was well again.

We did not treat the Gestapo searches very seriously until we had procured our first wireless, a battered crystal set that Harry had somehow managed to obtain and smuggle into the camp. The price, if I remember rightly, was a bar of chocolate, and the Pole who sold the set to Harry had the best of the bargain. We fiddled about with it for hours without success, beyond getting certain noises which certainly were not the B.B.C. As a set it was quite useless, but for a long time the mere possession of it gave us a lot of vicarious pleasure. The next Gestapo raid was indirectly responsible for its sudden disposal down the latrines.

One late afternoon Lober brought us news of their impending arrival.

'Another search,' the Kommandant sighed, as he came into the room. 'The Gestapo never let up.'

We watched him warily. Although we were grateful for the information, he had chosen a rather embarrassing moment to tell us. Only a few minutes before his arrival we had been fiddling with the crystal set, which was now back in its home in a Red Cross box. Unfortunately, the box was still on the table. And Lober had always shown that he had a strong curiosity about the contents of Red Cross boxes.

'We must make sure that the Gestapo find nothing when they come,' Lober was saying. And then his gaze fell on the Red Cross box. 'You prisoners live better than your jailers —really you do,' he said, stretching out his hand to lift the lid off the box. Before he had time to do so, Harry had snatched the box from the table and was clutching it protectively to his breast.

'Ah,' said Lober, with a broad wink. 'Contraband. A fine, fat rabbit, perhaps?'

Although Lober had shown that he was prepared to be broadminded about contraband, Harry knew perfectly well that he would take a pretty poor view of a wireless lying around the camp, even an obsolete model like ours.

'That's right,' Harry said. 'A rabbit.'

'You can trust me, boys,' Lober said cheerfully. 'Let's have a look at him.'

As he stretched out his hand for the box again, Harry quickly threw it over to me. As I caught it I saw the Kommandant's expression change.

'I want to see what is in that box,' he said loudly. He was no longer smiling.

Harry motioned to the door. As I went through it, I heard Harry rapidly explaining to Lober that it would be better if he didn't see the contents of the box, as he would then be able to face the Gestapo with a clear conscience.

As I stood in the latrines, disposing of the set bit by bit, I could hear Lober still roaring in our room. Suddenly all was quiet again. When I finally came out of the latrines, the Kommandant was walking towards the German barracks, a tin of cigarettes bulging from his pocket.

Soon after, we were able to obtain from the Poles a more modern wireless. This was brought up from the mine very much in the same way as the òne in the other camp. It was placed under a board in our room and brought out once a day for the news, which was taken down in shorthand and then read out to each barrack. From that time until the Russians were only a few kilometres away from our camp, we heard the news daily. During this period we had quite a number of visits from the Gestapo, but they never found it. So perhaps the Gestapo weren't so efficient, after all.

CHAPTER TEN

Kristina

ALTHOUGH the days were long since past when it was possible for a prisoner to keep a rendezvous in some dark alley, the barrack-rooms at night were still full of the talk of women. The talk was no longer bawdy, as it had been in the good old days, but sad and despairing. Now that the gates only opened and closed to let them go to and from the mine, the prisoners who had had *affaires* had begun to sentimentalize them, forgetting all the undignified scufflings that had gone on in the alley-ways while a guard smoked a cigarette and looked the other way. And the more I listened to them, the more I realized that even the illusion of love was better than nothing, and that I had been a fool in not having found a girl friend for myself.

None of us on the staff had taken advantage of the situation at the time, although we had been in the best position of all to do so. There had been no virtue in our restraint. Harry, as lord and master over two hundred men, had not wished to lower his prestige by joining in the general scramble, and Arthur and I had not thought it worth the risk of losing our jobs. Mac, the doctor, was in a different category. Perpetually engrossed in some book or other, he had hardly been aware of what had been going on.

I decided that it was not too late for me to do something about it. I was still allowed to go out for a walk whenever I wished, and if I could find a co-operative guard, there was no reason at all why I should not be as lucky as the others. I told Harry and Arthur of my intention, and they were definitely hostile towards the idea; not through any concern over my welfare, but because they knew that if I did meet someone, it would mean that I would begin making inroads into our Red Cross parcels, which we pooled for communal use.

For a long time I had no luck whatsoever. Half the old guards had been sent away, and those who remained had been thoroughly scared by dark remarks from Lober concerning traitor guards who deserved to be sent to a penal battalion or the Russian Front. Once it had got around what I was after, they practically fled at my approach.

It was Feldwebel Ernst Schmidt who finally helped me to find what I was seeking.

Schmidt was a Viennese, a genial giant of a man with the build of a boxer and the face of a Botticelli cherub. He had not been with us for very long, but he had dropped into the *Schreibstube* several times while I had been working there, and we had got on very well together. He had talked of Vienna and the marvellous *Gasthaus* which he owned there, and I had promised faithfully that if I ever went to Vienna after the war I would call in and see him.

Although we were on good terms, I had not tried to put to Schmidt the proposition I had been unsuccessfully hawking around to the other guards. Schmidt had seen a lot of action on various fronts, and he had made it quite clear from the beginning that he was not going to risk accelerating his return to one of them by helping prisoners in any illegal activities. He had even been dubious about letting in contraband from the mine, and it was not until Lober had spoken to him rather sharply on the matter that he had grudgingly allowed the prisoners to come into the camp without being searched.

Thirst was the indirect cause of Schmidt's fall from virtue. After he had been with us for some months, he began taking me for a walk every Saturday evening. We always took the same route: through the village and past the other camp, until we were on a quiet stretch of road with a solitary house in it. We would walk along this road and then turn down an unlighted passage-way that led into a deserted lane. Farther along there was the village *szynk*.[1] Every time we passed it, Schmidt would pause, and then rather regretfully continue walking. We did this for some weeks, and then one day Schmidt halted in the passage-way and said that would I mind waiting in the alley-way until he returned? Rather staggered, I agreed, and Schmidt departed, obviously quite confident that I would not take off in his absence. As I settled down to wait, I realized that he was not being so reckless as I had first thought. It was very unlikely that anyone would come up the passage-way, and if someone did, it would probably only be a Pole, who didn't count, anyway. Schmidt also knew that I would not attempt an escape from Poland without civilian clothes, food and a map; especially as I would probably be sent down the mine again if I were caught.

The alley-way was very dark and very quiet, and after I had been there for some time the almost unearthly silence began to unnerve me. Slowly, I walked to the top of the alley and looked across the road towards the solitary house —and as I did so I heard the sound of footsteps. I turned quickly and looked down the alley, thinking it was Schmidt returning. But the alley was deserted, and I realized that someone must be coming along the road. I shrank against the wall. The footsteps grew louder until at last I saw the dark outline of someone approaching. It was not until they were almost on top of me that I saw that it was a girl. I knew that if I stayed where I was she would see me lurking in the shadows and scream. Obviously the best thing for me to do was to show myself and hope for the best.

I stepped out into the road and said loudly: '*Dobry wieczor.*'[2]

The girl came to a halt and looked at me. Although there was a moon, I could not see her face clearly.

'*Angielski,*' I said. '*Angielski jeniec wojenny.*'[3] That was

[1] Pub. [2] Good evening. English prisoner-of-war.

about as much as I could manage in Polish. *'Habe kein angst,'* I said. *'Ich bin Englische Kreigsgefangene.'*

The girl came forward slowly until she was only a few paces from me. Now she had seen my uniform, she was smiling. She came even closer and we began to talk.

Her name was Kristina, she spoke English quite well, and by classical standards I suppose she was not beautiful. But as she stood there, talking softly to me, she struck me as being just about the most beautiful girl there was around Piaski. I had seen most of the photographs of the Polish girls the prisoners had met on their jaunts, and although the girls looked pleasant enough, they had all had that rather masculine bone structure that characterizes most Slav peasant types. Although there was only the moon to study Kristina by, I could see that she was slim and fair, and not at all like any of the girls I had seen in the photographs.

We walked slowly towards the house, and then stopped and talked in whispers so that the occupants of the house would not hear us, until finally she said it was time for her to go in. And then I kissed her and said that I would come again tomorrow, and would she please be sure to wait for me at the same time as this, for I would come whatever happened? She said she would and after she had gone into the house, I flung my forage-cap into the air and danced my way back to the alley to wait for Schmidt.

By the time he arrived, however, some of the exhilaration had worn off. I now had the problem of how to work it so that I could see Kristina tomorrow, and my only hope was Schmidt. But Schmidt, although a nice fellow, was not the type of man to consent to being a partner to the sort of thing I had in mind. All the way back to the camp I wanted to blurt out to Schmidt what had happened and then throw myself on his mercy. But instead, I remained silent, delaying for as long as possible the awful moment when he might say no to my pleadings. By the time we had reached the camp, I had decided to offer him as big a bribe as I could,

instead of trusting to friendship. I said to Schmidt that I
wanted to speak to him about the lists for next week's
shifts, but that I would have to collect the papers from my
room first.

Going to my room I raked out what cigarettes I had left
and also a bar of soap and, putting them into my pocket, I
went over to the *Schreibstube,* where Schmidt was impatiently waiting for me.

'Now what's the trouble about the lists?' he said.

'Never mind the lists,' I said. 'I want to speak to you
about something else.'

'Well?' Schmidt seemed tired and irritable and ready for
bed. I did not seem to have picked a good moment.

I took a deep breath. 'I want to go out again tomorrow
evening,' I said. 'To meet a girl.'

Schmidt stared. 'Are you mad?'

Then I told him what had happened. When I had
finished, I took the cigarettes and soap from my pocket and
placed them on the table.

'For you,' I said, 'if we go out for a walk tomorrow.'

Schmidt stared down at the table and shook his head
slowly.

'It's too dangerous,' he muttered.

'The house is right outside the village,' I said desperately.
'It's not dangerous—you *know* it is not dangerous.' I picked
up the cigarettes and soap and held them in front of him,
but he brushed them aside impatiently.

'No!'

I put the cigarettes and the soap back in my pocket, and
there was a long silence while we looked at each other across
the table.

'I thought you were my friend,' I said finally.

Schmidt frowned and said nothing.

'All right,' I said angrily. 'Let it be. But perhaps there
will come a time when I'm outside the wire and you behind
it. If it comes, I hope I will be one of the guards over you.'

'Quiet!' Schmidt looked anxiously towards the door. 'If

Lober ever heard you speaking like that, you would be working down the mine the next day.'

I was already feeling ashamed for what I had said. 'I am very sorry,' I said more quietly. 'I did not mean that.'

Schmidt shook his head wearily. 'You must understand. If we were caught, it would only mean a few days in the *bunker* for you. But for me . . .'

'I know,' I said. 'I'll go back to the camp now.'

Schmidt did not seem to hear the remark. 'I suppose,' he said thoughtfully, 'it must be very hard for all of you. No woman to love you for all that time.'

I had already reached the door. I stopped with my hand on the handle and waited.

'I don't know,' Schmidt said, 'I don't know what to say.'

'Tomorrow evening,' I said hopefully.

Schmidt hesitated and then his face broke into a broad grin. 'For you, I will do it.' He wagged a finger at me. 'But only once—and then it is finished.'

It was my turn to grin. 'Of course.'

I was about to leave the *Schreibstube,* when Schmidt called me back. 'You can leave the cigarettes and the soap,' he said dryly.

The next evening, the two of us checked out of the camp in the usual way, and with Schmidt breathing rather heavily at my side, I led the way towards the village. Schmidt was very quiet, and after a while I suddenly realized that he was suffering from a bad attack of the jitters. I could see that Schmidt was not really cut out for this sort of thing, and suddenly I had the awful feeling that if we were stopped for some routine questioning, his face would betray us immediately. What with Schmidt being frightened that the Gestapo might pounce on us and me being frightened of him giving the game away if that happened, the two of us must have made a pretty suspicious-looking pair as we slunk through the village.

But we did not even pass anyone in the streets, and at last we reached the top of the alley-way, near the house where Kristina lived. I caught Schmidt by the sleeve and pointed towards the house.

'I'm going in there,' I said.

'One hour, and no longer,' Schmidt said gruffly. 'And be careful.'

I watched him walking back down the alley-way. Then I turned and made my way slowly towards the house. As I did so, Kristina emerged from the shadows and came forward to meet me. Neither of us spoke for a moment.

'You see, I came,' I said finally.

She nodded but did not say anything, and then we began to walk slowly down the deserted lane. When we were in front of the house, I made a movement towards the gate. But Kristina quickly caught me by the arm and began to steer me past the house.

'Not in the house,' she said. 'The people below are almost strangers, and it might be dangerous.'

We walked down the lane, until at last we were standing in a large field at the back of the house. We walked around the field for some time, and then I took off my overcoat and placed it on the ground and we laid down upon it. But it was too cold there, even for us, and we got up and began walking again.

'I don't see why we can't go into the house,' I said savagely. 'The other people in the house are Poles, aren't they? They won't betray us.'

I kept nagging on in this strain for some while, and in the end Kristina took me back to the house. Very quietly we crept up the stairs and entered her room. It was small and poky, with not much furniture in it; there was a small table with a lighted oil-lamp on it, and in the outlying shadows around the table a crude wooden cupboard, a few chairs, a small sink, a bed, and a gas-ring, and that was all.

We were both cold from walking around the field, especially Kristina, for the clothes she wore were thin and threadbare, and for some time I sat on the edge of the bed with her, rubbing her hands, trying to get them warm. Then I looked at the clock and saw that the hour was already up, and much as I wanted to stay for just a little while longer, I knew that I had to go.

'I must go now,' I said. 'If I keep the guard waiting, he will not let me come again.'

We lay back on the bed for a few minutes, and then I got up and left.

Now that I had visited Kristina once without any trouble it was not difficult to persuade Schmidt to make a weekly jaunt of it. Each time I went up to see her, I took with me something from my Red Cross parcel. I tried to spread the gifts out so that I took something different each week—chocolate, coffee, and butter one week, a pair of woollen gloves, a tin of meat, and some biscuits the following week, and so on. It used to give me a great deal of pleasure just to sit there, watching her almost childlike delight as she struggled with the knots of the parcel that I had so carefully wrapped up for her.

Entering that poky little room was like entering another world. After the years of lying, stealing, fighting, and scrounging, I had come to the stage where I was mentally as hard as nails, and altogether not a very nice person to know. In that room, I learnt, if nothing else, to be kind again, and in a way it rather spoilt me for looking after myself afterwards in the jungle of prison life.

The visits to Kristina went on for weeks, until one day Lober called Schmidt into his office. From what I gathered from Schmidt afterwards, Lober had been very pleasant. He had asked Schmidt how he liked it at the camp, and Schmidt said that he liked it very much, and how pleasant he found it working with Lober. Lober had said that he was very pleased to hear it, and then had gone on to tell Schmidt of all the trouble he had had in the past with the guards. He hoped that Schmidt would never be tempted to be so foolish as they had been. The consequences could be very serious. And with that, Lober dismissed him.

It was obvious that Lober had smelt a rat. I suppose it

had suddenly occurred to him that it was rather strange that I should want to go out, week after week, after having spent months in the camp without showing any particular desire for exercise.

Schmidt took the hint and the visits to Kristina ceased. For some days after I mooned around the camp, the picture of misery. When I could stand it no longer, I escaped. 'Escaped' is perhaps too dramatic a word for it. Late one Saturday evening, I finished off the work lists, laid them carefully on the table, and then walked out of the German barrack. Instead of going towards the gate, I sidled around the barrack and disappeared into the darkness. It was as easy as that. No one saw me go.

I skirted around the village, keeping to the fields, until at last I was standing behind the house. There was a light showing through a chink in Kristina's curtains, and picking up a pebble, I threw it at her window. She must have known immediately that it was me, for she did not even bother to look out of the window, but came down at once. We stood talking together for a few minutes, and then went into the house.

The next morning when I awoke, I looked at Kristina sleeping beside me, and I knew that I had made a mistake.

When she awoke I said: 'I think I have been very wrong in coming to you. It was not so dangerous for you when I came for a single hour. But now that I have escaped, it is different. They will be looking for me everywhere.'

She smiled up from the pillow, but said nothing.

'They shave the hair off the heads of German women who go with prisoners,' I said. 'But they won't be so kind to you.'

She shrugged her shoulders and then clambered out of the bed. I watched her for some time while she prepared coffee. Then I said without much conviction: 'I think I should go back before they find me here.'

'Stay,' she said. 'And don't worry for me.'

So I stayed. Early every morning, Kristina would go off to

work in some factory on the outskirts of Sosnowiec, and I would settle down to await her return. The hours of waiting meant hours spent at the window looking out across the great stretches of snow-covered fields, while I thought of what would happen to Kristina if the Gestapo found me in the house. And then she would come home late at night, and we would go to bed and everything would be all right again for a few hours. But in the early morning, while Kristina slept beside me, I would begin thinking again. There were three days and nights of this, and then on the fourth day I decided that it could not go on any longer. For once I did not look forward to hearing Kristina's key in the front door.

I had wanted to say what had to be said as soon as she came in. But I found it almost impossible to do so, and instead I went and sat down quietly at the table while Kristina heated some soup on the gas-ring and put the bread on the table. I decided that I would say it after the meal, and for the rest of the time made conversation with my heart in my stomach.

When the meal was over, we sat quietly on the edge of the bed, our shadows large against the wall from the oil-lamp that stood on the table. I knew that if we sat there much longer, we would turn out the lamp and get into bed and it would begin all over again. Another day in the room, more self-recriminations, and it all ending in the same place—the bed.

I jumped up and said harshly: 'I am going back to the camp.'

She looked up, puzzled, and I knew that she thought that she had misunderstood me.

'I'm leaving, Kristina,' I said. 'Going back to the camp.'

She got up slowly from the bed. 'You no longer love me?'

'Of course I do,' I said. 'It's not that. I just can't stay here any more. It was very selfish of me to come here in the first place. You know that if they find me here, it would be very bad for you.'

She ignored that. 'Don't go,' she said quietly.

I knew the worst part of it was coming now.

'I must go,' I said. 'And tonight. And in a few minutes. Or I shall never go.'

'Not tonight,' she said. 'Tomorrow, if you must, but not tonight.'

Just for a moment I smiled. 'No, Kristina,' I said. 'Another night won't make me change my mind, so it's still better that I should go now.'

Going over to the door, I took my overcoat off the peg. Then I came back to her.

'After the war I will come back,' I said. 'I promise.' I took her hand. It felt very cold, and I suddenly remembered the first time I had come into this room and spent my precious hour trying to warm her hands.

'No,' she said, taking her hand away. 'You will not come back.'

'After the war,' I said. 'I promise. I promise.'

There were some tears, but not so many as to make it unbearable, and quite suddenly I found that the worst was over and all that was left for me to do was to get out of the room.

'Good-bye, Kristina,' I said. I kissed her, but too hard and without too much feeling, because it was easier for me that way.

I broke away and went out of the room quickly, closing the door behind me. As I ran down the stairs I heard the door open on the landing, and looking up I saw Kristina leaning over the banister. I waved, stood in the passage for a moment, and then went outside and closed the front door softly behind me.

On my arival back at the camp, there was an immediate inquest in Lober's office. Lober kept banging on the table, and demanded to know who the Pole was who had been sheltering me. Schmidt stood beside me, silent and worried-looking. When I told Lober that I had no intention of telling him anything, there was more shouting, more fist-pounding on the table, and threats of being handed over to the Gestapo if I did not speak. Finally, Lober calmed down.

'Take him to the *bunker*,' Lober said wearily. 'And keep him there until I say he can come out.'

I was marched off to 'solitary'. For several days I stayed locked up in a room without light and living on bread and water, and then suddenly I was out again, and not only out, but back on my old job.

Lober now seemed anxious to forget the whole business as quickly as possible. I suppose he had realized that if he made too much fuss about the matter, he might bring the Gestapo on the scene. Any investigations on their part could have led to a number of things coming to light which would not exactly help Lober's military career. A Kommandant who had been discovered allowing his guards to be bribed and his camp turned into a zoo would have had an uncertain future, to say the least of it.

But it was some time before all was forgiven and I was allowed to go out walking again, and then only under the strictest supervision. On one of these occasions I saw Kristina; we smiled across the road at each other and then went our different ways. After that, I never saw her again.

CHAPTER ELEVEN

'The Long Road Home'

LIKE so many other prisoners, I had long ago adjusted myself to the idea that I might have to spend the rest of my life behind the wire. Although this was a defeatist attitude to take, surprisingly enough it did make life much simpler. One lived for the day and the simple pleasures that one could get out of it, instead of always pining for the past. Having reached this frame of mind, I had found the continual and, needless to say, false rumours merely irritating instead of helpful; the news of the small victories gained in the desert merely an extension of a war we were going to lose, anyway, and letters from home only a painful reminder of a world outside which we might never see again.

The wireless, of course, was to blame. Without it we could have fed on the febrile latrine rumours that were brought into camp each day. But there had been no escape from the inexorable voice of the B.B.C. announcer. Although the wireless might have helped us to feel that we were cocking a snoot at the Germans, in the end it defeated its purpose and brought us to despair as we listened glumly to it, night after night, while it poured out the depressing details of the continual Allied defeats. When the news had changed for the better and we were able to follow Rommel's defeat in the desert, we were only mildly interested. The desert was a long way from Europe, and in the end it did not seem to us that it was going to make much difference.

D-Day had been quite another matter, and for some months we had lived in a state of feverish excitement, while the Allied troops battled their way across France. But then the winter came, the Germans broke through the Ardennes, and once more the end seemed far away. For most of us in

Piaski, the days and the weeks and the months merged into a quiet pattern of life governed by food, cigarettes, and books.

It was not until the Allied Forces had crossed the Rhine and the Russians were sweeping across Poland that we knew that at last the end was in sight.

When the Russians finally began to approach our mining village, there was a lot of excited surmise as to what the Germans would do with us. It seemed to us there were only two alternatives: either they would put us on a train that would take us to another camp in the heart of Germany, or they would leave us to the Russians. Frankly, no one seemed very keen on being left to the Russians. The Germans were a known quantity, and the Russians were not. The steady dose of propaganda we had been given regarding 'The Russian Beasts' had taken partial root, and we were definitely in favour of the idea of packing our kitbags and departing with the Germans.

At this period we had no idea of what was really in store for us; that the Germans would take us out on the roads and keep us on them for nearly four months, trudging through the snow and icy winds, with our ranks being thinned out all the time by frostbite, starvation, death at the hands of the Germans, and, finally, death from our own planes.

All that we knew at that time was that the Russians *were* coming to Piaski, for we had already heard in the far distance the continual muffled thudding of their guns. The next day the sound of the guns was much nearer, and the following night everyone was at the windows looking up at the sky, illuminated from time to time by a bright light as the Russian artillery banged away, shaking our flimsy wooden barracks. We knew then that, in a matter of a couple of days at the most, we would either be in the hands of the Russians or on our way to Germany.

Actually, our departure from Piaski began late that night. As I stood there looking out of the staff-room window, the gates of the camp opened and the guards poured into the compound yelling for everyone to get on parade. For once we actually hurried to obey the guards' orders. As we streamed out, the Russian artillery was banging away even harder than ever. Standing in the snow outside, waiting for us, was the tall, angular form of the Kommandant. Lober watched us morosely as we lined up, his mouth jerking slightly each time a fresh burst from the guns shook the buildings around us. Finally, he moved forward and began to speak.

'As you will no doubt have gathered, the Russians are coming.' Although he was shouting, we could only just hear him speaking above the barrage. 'We have just been told that all prisoners in this area are to be evacuated immediately. We leave this camp at dawn. You will take as much food with you as possible, and as many blankets as you can carry.' He looked at us grimly. 'You realize that if we left you here, the Russians would probably kill you on sight. Fortunately for you, the German Reich has always been concerned with the welfare of the prisoners in its charge, and even in this moment of crisis has not forgotten you.'

Someone sniggered and then fell silent as Lober glowered at him. Actually, although I felt that Lober was overdoing it a little, like everyone else, I had no inclination to be around when the fighting started in Piaski. We were, in fact, just as anxious to get moving as Lober and the guards were. Only one thing bothered me as I went back to my room to pack. The Kommandant had said nothing of where we were going and how we were going to get there.

We were all outside the camp when the dawn came and, muffled to the nose with scarves and balaclavas, we shuffled our feet in a vain attempt to keep them warm while we waited for the guards to count us off. As we stood there in the biting wind on that January morning, with the snow scurrying around us in great flakes, I think that most of us felt that for the first time in five years we were in sight of home again. While we were being counted, the other working party from up the road joined us and was tacked on to the rear of our column.

Finally, after innumerable recounts, the guards arrived at the correct total, and we began to shuffle off down the road with Lober in charge of the lot of us. As we did so, the deserted street suddenly became alive with Poles, who came out of their cottages and the side roads to line the street and wave us a silent farewell. It was a sad moment for us. For a long time, almost a lifetime it seemed, we had worked side by side with many of them, looked at their photographs, talked of their family life and our own lives before the war, and been made to feel by them that we were still part of the outside world. Now we would never see them again. If we ever reached our own homes, not only the Continent would separate us, but also a way of life that would seem, in retrospect, like a dream. Suddenly, I thought of Kristina again, and began to look for her among the small groups on each side of the road. But she wasn't there, and somehow it didn't seem to matter much, anyway. The meeting and the events which followed had had an unreal quality from the beginning.

We trailed out of the village and into the open countryside, where the icy wind swept across the fields with such force that we were hardly able to keep a foothold on a road that was like glass.

Later that morning the wind dropped, and almost at the same time the Russian guns also stopped. An oppressive silence hung over the Polish countryside as we trudged on. Suddenly someone began to sing one of the more ribald army songs, and soon the whole column took it up. As the guards made no attempt to stop us, we kept this up for some time, until at last the effort of walking through the snow silenced the lot of us. No one seemed particularly worried about the future. The general assumption was that we were heading for another working party, where we would be linked up with other prisoners, and then put on a train that would take us to some camp in the heart of Germany.

Our first day on the road was fairly uneventful, and at about six o'clock that evening we landed up outside Beuthen, where we were herded into some huts that had obviously been previously occupied by some British prisoners-of-war. It was evident that they had left in a hurry. Torn letters lay on the floor, together with odd bits of clothing, Red Cross cartons, and empty tins. On the walls had been scribbled the usual Anglo-Saxon words, together with a few pithy remarks about Hitler and the Germans. All of us were starving hungry, and as soon as we had got settled, most of us dived into our kit-bags for a tin. Although we had had hourly breaks on the road, none of us had been able to force ourselves to fumble with a tin-opener while we stood around stamping our feet, waiting for the order to move again. After sharing a tin of cold, rubbery luncheon meat with Arthur, I clambered up on one of the bunks and fell asleep instantly.

When we straggled out on to the road at dawn the next day, I personally was beginning to feel worried. No sign of other prisoners, no sign of a railway, no information about where we were heading; only a long, white road, stretching into the wilderness ahead of us. We marched from dawn until late evening and then, to crown it all, we landed up at a small farm, where we were herded into a number of out-houses, open at the front and with great holes in the roofs. With suitable apologies for the accommodation, Lober and most of the guards departed for the warmth of the farm-house.

After that, the days went by like a continuous nightmare. Every day we staggered along the frozen roads or across fields, up to our knees in snow, hoping that the night would bring us some warm shelter. But it never did. Every night we landed up at some desolate farm, standing bleakly in the middle of a snowy waste, and every night there was a fight for the warmest places. If it was a small farm, a lucky few would be able to get in with the pigs in the pig-sties—if it was a larger farm, there was always the cowshed which could accommodate quite a number. The rest slept in barns and buried themselves beneath straw in a futile attempt to find warmth from the winds that blew in through the countless cracks and crannies.

Starting off in the mornings was sheer agony, for overnight one's boots had frozen into great solid hunks of leather, as stiff as wood, and to move in them was an excruciating torture that was eased only after some hours of marching.

For the first week or so we circled aimlessly around Upper Silesia. It was obvious that our route was being worked out day by day, according to whatever reports Lober received as to the position of the Russians. From the way we had gone, first one way and then another, we gathered that the Russians were coming in from all directions. Finally, Lober made up his mind which way he was going to take us, and the column crossed into Sudetenland.

A few days after we had left Upper Silesia, I parted company with the rest of the staff. We had been quarrelling among ourselves on and off since we had left the camp, and at last I got sick of it. A final violent quarrel about food brought things to a head, and leaving them I elbowed myself into a place farther up the column.

The food from our Red Cross parcels was running low, although all had conserved as much as possible when they had seen what they were in for. We had received no food from the Germans, but finally we were issued with some soup-powder and dehydrated meat. That night I slept in a stable with a decrepit horse, which ferreted the lot out of my kit-bag while I was asleep. Not content with that, he also finished off my last packet of biscuits.

The next morning I wandered out into the yard, where some of the prisoners were boiling up their soup-powder and dehydrated meat over the few small fires that the guards had allowed them to make. I stood there for a moment, thinking of my rations now in the stomach of a horse, and then slowly wandered over to one of the fires. After a suitable interval of casual watching, I bent down over one of the tins, while its owner watched me suspiciously. I breathed in deeply, and then stood up again, looking like one of the Bisto kids.

'Smells delicious,' I said.

The owner of the can grunted.

I coughed and then said: 'A horse stole my rations in the night. I'd be very interested in finding out if that tastes as delicious as it smells.'

'F—— off,' the owner of the can said succinctly.

I retreated to the stable to tackle one of my last tins of luncheon meat. The pattern of the march from France was already beginning to repeat itself.

Soon after that we began to come across the German refugees, streaming westwards, creating great bottle-necks on the frozen roads. There were families struggling to move handcarts piled high with furniture; peasant women standing stoically at the sides of the roads with shapeless bundles on their backs, and cars with their engines frozen up, their owners fuming helplessly as they watched the hundreds on foot struggling past them through the slush. The Russian guns, still booming at odd intervals, sounded nearer than ever.

In the end we were taken off the main roads and led across fields and down quiet country lanes that took us even farther from civilization, until there was nothing in sight but the occasional bush or tree standing black and stark against the dazzling whiteness of the snow.

Eventually we began to come across other columns of British prisoners, also moving westward. It was not long before we loathed the very sight of them. Other prisoners on our route could mean their taking all the available accommodation for the night, leaving us only the fields to sleep in. But of course, on those occasions we did not sleep, but instead, circled aimlessly around the field until dawn, hoping that our blood would keep circulating enough to keep off frostbite. The Kommandant was with his guards in the one and only house nearby. As the guards took turns in coming out to watch over us, there was no question of escaping. Fortunately, nights like these were rare, and after them the evenings spent huddled against some pig in its sty seemed positive luxury, lice and all.

Our main source of food was now potatoes scrounged from the farms. In the evenings, we would gather in the yard of a farm, and huddle in little groups around the fires we had made to cook our potatoes. While some of us tried to keep the fires going, other prisoners went around searching for wood, generally almost pulling the farm down in the process. There was the usual hysterical screaming from the guards; shots fired into the air and threats of dire punishment. But the fires were kept going, just the same. The guards at that time were not so vicious as they were to become later, when most of Western Germany was being overrun by our own troops.

Although most of the farmers took a poor view of our raids on their poultry and our desperate attempts to pull down their outhouses for wood, there were others who were friendly and sympathetic and who tried to help us by giving us hot water and by boiling up great bowls of potatoes, which they shared out among us.

But it was not always a farm in which we landed up for the night. There was a barrel factory, for instance. Arriving late one afternoon in a small isolated village, we were led to the entrance of a large brick building.

'You're lucky,' Lober said, pointing to the building. 'You have good accommodation for the night. I sent two guards on in advance to find this place, and they went to a lot of trouble to find somewhere comfortable for you. I hope you are grateful.'

No one looked particularly appreciative. The building had one stout door and no windows. It was the sort of place where they could lock us up for the night, and forget about us till morning, without even the trouble of posting guards. It also looked very cold.

As we went into the building, we had a brief glimpse of innumerable wooden casks and planks of wood. The door was slammed on us and we were in complete darkness. For a while we stumbled around blindly, trying to find a suitable place to settle down for the night. Occasionally, someone would strike a precious match and a small corner of the building would be lit up to reveal some haggard, unshaven prisoner trying to settle himself in a barrel or on a plank of wood. The floor was of concrete, and therefore untenable.

As the night went on, the building became colder. As we had filed into the place, the guards had warned us that on no account were we to start up any fires. With no windows in the place, no means of exit in a case of emergency, and precious little ventilation, common sense told us that for once we would be wise to obey them.

As I fumbled around in the darkness, looking for a place to sleep, my hand suddenly landed on a bald head. The aggrieved voice that told me, with the addition of the usual army terms, to take my hand away, belonged to Spot Read. Wearily, I sank down on the cement floor beside him.

'All this lovely wood,' Spot said beside me. 'We could make a wonderful fire.' He was suddenly silent again, and I could almost hear him brooding in the darkness.

'We *will* have a fire, and ―― 'em,' Spot said suddenly. 'Got any matches?'

Rather doubtfully, I produced a box and struck one. For a moment Spot's large and battered face beamed at me, and then we were in darkness again.

'This is going to be a bit dangerous, isn't it?' I said.

Spot's further remarks are not printable. A few moments later we were busy collecting wood shavings and any available timber small enough to put on a fire. Not to be outdone, other prisoners began doing the same thing. Some time later, about a dozen fires were well on the way, and becoming more ambitious we put whole barrels on them. Basking in the heat, we ignored the thick, choking smoke that was rapidly filling the whole of the building.

The next morning when the door was opened, we staggered out with blackened faces and red-rimmed eyes, and took great gulps of the cold air down into our aching lungs. The smoke from the still-smouldering fires billowed out gently behind us.

Lober watched it with fascinated horror for a moment, and then, grabbing a rifle from the nearest guard, he began to lay into us like a man possessed. While we hopped and ran backwards and forwards in the snow, avoiding the Kommandant's swipes, one of the guards kept saying something about the owner of the factory arriving shortly. Eventually the remark penetrated Lober's brain, and the next moment we were going out of the village at the double, with Lober still busy with the rifle butt.

Soon after that incident we learned that our final destination was Bavaria. Bavaria! Someone worked out that it was over three hundred miles away as the crow flies. With the route we were taking, it would be over four hundred miles, if we ever made it. By the way things were going, it didn't seem as if we would.

By now our food had completely run out. Fortunately, most of us had brought extra clothing with us, and this we bartered with the farmers. A pair of long underpants or two pairs of woollen socks, Red Cross issue, would be handed over for half a loaf and perhaps a small piece of sausage. After all the clothing had gone, our watches, pens, and other personal belongings went the same way—generally to the guards.

After that things really became desperate. The cold and the lack of food turned a lot of the men into something almost like wild beasts. Men fought over the swill buckets in the farms, robbed each other, and begged on the farmers' doorsteps with sickening servility. Survival at all costs was the order of the day. Nothing else mattered.

On top of all this, quite a number of men at last began to develop frost-bite in their toes and fingers, and sometimes in the nose. They were not a very pleasant sight, and as usual with this sort of thing, the Germans were in no hurry to see that they were given treatment. Whenever someone developed frost-bite, he had to wait until he had walked to some place that was large enough to have a hospital where he could be left. The route we were taking did not touch many places like that.

The smartness that we had prided ourselves on so much at the camp was now a thing of the past. We were only able to wash ourselves in the snow, or occasionally allowed to dip into one of the buckets of water that the villagers were in the habit of leaving by the roadside for us. Fortunately, it was too cold for lice to take hold, and for that we were duly grateful.

Then something happened which gave us fresh heart. For some days we had heard rumours from the guards that we would soon be receiving Red Cross parcels again. Even in our wildest wishful thinking we had not thought of this, and we dismissed it as something that the guards had cooked up to keep us going. But one bleak afternoon, soon after dusk, a fleet of vans with the Red Cross insignia on them suddenly passed us and made for the village where we were due to stay the night. The Red Cross, which had done so much for us in the past, had come to the rescue again. When we arrived at the village the parcels were waiting for us, stacked in great heaps by the roadside. There was no sign of the Red Cross vans.

As the first parcels had to be shared between three men, combines were formed again, then and there, more or less with one's immediate neighbours. Strangely enough, I found myself beside Spot Read once more.

'You might as well come in with me,' he said. 'You need someone to look after you, anyway.'

'I've been doing pretty well,' I said with dignity.

'You're hopeless,' Spot said. 'Anyway, I'm not arguing. You're going into partnership with me.'

And that more or less settled it. For the third member of the combine, we eventually settled on a lugubrious-looking prisoner named Parsons who, although perhaps not very smart, could be trusted not to run off with the food as soon as our backs were turned.

Carrying our parcel into the farm where we were to sleep, the three of us made for the barn and then clambered up a ladder and into the hay-loft. Then we squatted down and just looked at the parcel. Spot cut the string. We lifted the lid, peered at the contents, and then Spot put the lid on again.

'We eat just before we go to bed,' Spot said. 'But first of all, Vincent and me are going to look round the farm. We might be able to get at the potato store. Just because we've got this parcel, it doesn't mean we can afford to slacken off. You can stay here and guard the parcel, Parsons.'

It certainly seemed to be our lucky day. Soon after we had left the barn, we found a store of seed potatoes in a small shed in a corner of the yard.

We returned to the parcel to find Parsons missing.

'The parcel!' Spot cried. 'He's pinched it.'

'That doesn't sound like Parsons,' I said. 'Let's have a look round in the straw. Maybe he's hidden it there.'

We searched the straw in vain.

Spot was swearing softly to himself when Parsons's head appeared over the edge of the loft.

'Sorry,' Parsons said breathlessly. 'Had to go off and have a pee.' He stood on the ladder and smiled up at us uncertainly.

Spot sighed with audible relief and then looked at Parsons severely. 'You gave us a nasty shock. When we couldn't find the parcel, we thought you'd gone off with it. Thank goodness, you had the sense to take it with you.'

Something in the expression on Parsons's face suddenly gave me a nasty sick feeling in the stomach. I leaned over the edge of the loft to see if Parsons had anything in his other hand. It was empty.

'Didn't you take it with you?' I said hoarsely.

Parsons shook his head dumbly, and then clambered up on to the platform beside me.

Spot stared at him. 'Do you mean to say you just went off and left it here?' For a moment I thought Spot was going to hit him.

Rather inadequately, Parsons said: 'I'm sorry.'

'It's no good,' I said. 'It's gone, and that's the end of it. God knows when we'll see another one.'

We both looked at Parsons. 'You know what you are, don't you?' Spot said, and immediately proceeded to tell him.

After that, Parsons was summarily dismissed from the combine, while Spot and I went outside to make a fire in which to bake our seed potatoes. A few days later we rather regretted Parsons's banishment, especially when we found out he had had a watch which he had bartered for three loaves. Spot attempted a reconciliation, and seemed surprised when it was spurned.

Fortunately we received another parcel about a week later. After that, we received one each about every ten days or so. It wasn't much to live on, but it was just enough. Without those parcels, I don't think many of us would have survived the march. This distribution of parcels did not apply to the Russian prisoners on the march, who were not allowed to receive them. As usual, the Germans were making sure that the Russians had as little chance as possible of survival.

If we felt that we were hard done by on that march, we were soon to realize that we were lucky compared with the Russian prisoners. It was not until we started going over the *Riesengebirge* into Czechoslovakia that we came across them on the march. We had known several days before that a column must be only a little way ahead of us, for we had come across their bodies lying by the roadside, frozen stiff in grotesque attitudes, often with a bullet in their heads or in their backs. We were not very surprised or even shocked at these sights, for we knew only too well how the Russians were treated.

We began clambering the steep, winding roads over the

Riesengebirge early one morning. Fortunately, the snow had begun to fall again, covering the frozen roads with a fine powder that enabled us to keep a foothold on them. But it was slow going, and every so often we were forced to halt. Each time we halted I looked below at the great expanse of lifeless countryside, and consoled myself with the thought that at least it would not be long before I would be out of Germany for a while.

About midday we caught up with the Russian column. They were like skeletons in scarecrow clothing, their bones poking through their torn and tattered clothes that flapped around them in the wind. Their eyes were big and round, and quite dead as they stared at us from their sunken faces. As they struggled through the snow, the guards bellowed and laid into them all the time with their rifle butts. Even as we passed, a Russian prisoner fell out of the column and lay twitching in the snow. A guard was on him immediately, lashing at his head and shoulders with his gun butt. Quite suddenly a growl went up from the whole column of British prisoners. It was quite spontaneous, and the sound of it, was I suppose, quite frightening. The guard stopped, his rifle poised in the air. Then, without so much as another look at the Russian on the ground, he stepped over him and followed the Russian column. As I passed the Russian on the ground, I saw that he was already dead.

The next day, for the first time, the sun came out, and for the first time since we had left the camp we took off our balaclavas and gloves, and walked with our coats open. We were now in Czechoslovakia, and already most of us had the feeling that better times were ahead. The first village we had gone through had been lined with people who had thrown us cigarettes and biscuits. The guards had not interfered or said much, but they had not been very pleased at the reception we received.

The weather became warmer with every passing day; the villagers continued to be friendly, and threw us food whenever they could; and the Czech farmers with whom we stayed at night filled us with potatoes and soup and told us the news they had heard on the radio. The terrors of the march seemed over. Now all we had to do was keep marching, going through the villages like visiting royalty, graciously accepting the gifts that the population chose to shower on us.

But, of course, it was too good to last. We had underestimated the guards. Familiarity had bred a good-natured contempt, and we got to the stage where we thought we could get away with anything at the cost of a bawling out or an occasional blow across the shoulders with a rifle butt. We should have known better. During the next few days, as the news got progressively worse for the Germans on the Western Front, with Patton's Army swallowing up places where some of the guards had their homes, they became sour and so strict that it soon became impossible for us to step out of the column to take any of the titbits or cigarettes that the Czechs offered us. Even Schmidt, who had been on good terms with most of the prisoners, was sullen and irritable and given to fits of almost insane anger. The only difference was that he never actually struck anyone.

Things came to a head a few days later. We were passing quietly through a village, when suddenly a Czech woman darted into the road, holding out a packet of cigarettes to one of the prisoners. As he stepped out of the column to take it, a red-haired guard ran quickly forward and shot him through the head. The whole thing happened so quickly that I found myself passing the crumpled body in the road before I had fully realized what had happened. We marched on in silence, shaken and suddenly very frightened. Behind us the woman sobbed softly by the roadside.

That first shot seemed to set off a new mood for the march. Guards hammered prisoners with rifle butts or shot them down on the slightest pretext, until in the end one started off the day wondering if one were going to finish it alive. Everyone was very careful indeed how he behaved, but despite our caution there were still casualties. Fortunately, after a while things eased up a little, and everything was more or less as it had been before—unless, of course, you were unwise enough to try to take any of the food and cigarettes offered you by the Czechs. Finally, pamphlets were distributed over the area we were marching through, telling the population that under no circumstances were they to give us food.

However, I would be unfair if I said that there was no kindness ever shown by any of the guards towards the prisoners. There were a few who would always share what little bread they had to spare. On one occasion, a guard who saw me trying to sell a pair of socks, seemed quite upset by the fact—so much so that he gave me a loaf of bread on the spot. This sudden sentimentality was a little surprising, however, as he must have been aware that hunger was not new to me on that march.

Half-way across Czechoslovakia, the Germans distributed among us some incredible pamphlets. A copy of this pamphlet is reproduced on the next page.

This, of course, was not the first time they had tried to recruit prisoners-of-war into the German Army. At one time a British Free Corps had been established by them, and although it met with no real success, I'm sorry to say that it did get volunteers. The Germans had tried to find recruits for it by going around to the working parties to find out who were the good workers there. These were sent to a so-called rest-camp as a reward for working hard for the German Reich. Once there, everything had been laid on for them. Plenty of sport, films, trips to the local village dances, and a life of general ease were all part of the softening-up process. After a spell of this, it was suggested that they might like to join the British Free Corps. Not to fight against their own troops, but against the Russians. Most of the men gladly accepted the vacation at the holiday camp and turned down the rest. But there were exceptions. The pamphlet is perhaps interesting in the light of recent events, but to us at the time it seemed to be only the result of some ridicu-

Soldiers of the British Commonwealth!

Soldiers of the United States of America!

The great Bolshevik offensive has now crossed the frontiers of Germany. The men in the Moscow Kremlin believe the way is open for the conquest of the Western world. This will certainly be the decisive battle for us. But it will also be the decisive battle for England, for the United States and for the maintenance of Western civilisation.

Or whatever today remains of it.

The events in the Baltic States, in Poland, Hungary and Greece are proof enough for us all to see the real program behind the mask of Moscow's socalled **"limited national aims"** and reveals to us how Moscow interprets democratic principles both for the countries she has conquered and also for Germany and **for your countries as well.**

It is also clear enough **today** that the issue at stake is not merely the destruction of Germany and the extermination of the German race. **The fate of your country too is at stake.** This means the fate of your wives, of your children, your home. It also means everything that make life livable, lovable and honorable for you.

Each one of you who has watched the development of Bolshevism throughout this war knows in his innermost heart the truth about Bolshevism. Therefore we are now addressing you as white men to other white men. This is not an appeal. At least we feel there is no alternative for any of us, who feels himself a citizen of our continent and our civilisation but to stop the red flood here and now.

Extraordinary events demand extraordinary measures and decisions. One of these decisions is now put up to you. We address ourselves to you regardless of your rank or of your nationality.

Soldiers We are sure there are some amongst you who have recognized the danger of Bolshevik-Communism for his own country. We are sure that many of you have seen clearly what this war is now leading to. **We are sure that many of you see what the consequences of the destruction of Europe — not just of Germany but of Europe — will mean to your own country.** Therefore we want to make the following proposal to all of you.

We think that our fight has also become your fight. If there are some amongst you who are willing to take consequences and who are willing to join the ranks of the German soldiers who fight in this battle which will decide both the fate of Germany and the fate of your countries we should like to know it. We invite you to join our ranks and the tens of thousands of volunteers from the communist crushed and conquered nations of eastern Europe, which have had to choose between submission under an most brutal asiatic rule — or a national existence in the future under European ideas, many of which, of course are your own ideals.

Whether you are willing to fight in the front-line or in the service corps: we make you this solemn promise: Whoever as a soldier of his own nation is willing to join the common front for the common cause, will be freed immediately after the victory of the present offensive and can return to his own country via Switzerland.

All that we have to ask from you is the word of the gentleman not to fight directly or indirectly for the cause of Bolshivik-Communism so long as this war continues.

At this moment we do not ask you to think about Germany. We ask you to think about your own country, we ask you just to measure the chaos which you and your people at home would have to, in case the Bolshivik-Communism onslaught should overpower Europe. We must and we will put an end to Bolshevism and we will achieve this under all circumstances. Please inform the convoy-officer of your decision and you will receive the privileges of our own men for we expect you to share their duty. This is something which surpasses all national boundaries. The world today is confronted by the fight of the east against the west. We ask you to think it over.

Are you for the culture of West or the barbaric asiatic East?

Make your decision now!

lous wishful thinking at high level. It was not treated very seriously by the guards, either, who handed out the pamphlets in the most perfunctory manner, together with some appropriate jokes as to what to do with them.

Some time later we went out of Czechoslovakia into Southern Germany. Quite often now, we could see far above us our own planes. At that time they were an encouraging sight—a link with the forces that were going to liberate us.

A few days after we had crossed into Southern Germany, we were put into a disused railway station and told that we were going to stay there for a week. Working parties would be sent out from there, when and wherever they were needed. It seemed that we were now killing time until the end.

The next day a working party was sent out to some large railway sidings, about ten miles away. The working party returned that evening to report that planes had come over and then flown off again. When the party was due to go off there again the next day, Schmidt asked if I would like to go with the party as interpreter—a tin of meat being the bait. Remembering the planes that were over the sidings the day before, I declined. Late that night, the working party returned with hair-raising tales of narrow escapes while American planes came down and machine-gunned the sidings. Fortunately there were no casualties.

The day after that we had an attack on the railway station where we were billeted. We were standing around in little groups, chatting quite happily, when suddenly the air was full of the roar of engines and the chatter of machine-guns. Everyone fell flat on his face. As I was one of the first down, I found myself beneath about a dozen men, and very grateful to be there. When we clambered to our feet again, we saw two planes streaking away from us. Again there were no casualties—unless you could count those unfortunates who had dived into the latrine pits.

We were more than grateful when we moved the next day.

Soon afterwards we reached Regensburg. It was a really beautiful day, and as we stopped within sight of the town, Spot and I sat down by the banks of the Danube. I was feeling more relaxed and contented than I had done for a long time. It was a pleasant spot, with the waters swirling past us on one side, and a small wood on the other side of us, leading up to a railway line. In front of us, about a hundred yards away, was a railway bridge that led over to Regensburg.

'You know,' I said, settling comfortably, 'I think we're going to make it. I really do.'

Spot spat in the river. 'We're not free yet. Not by a long chalk.' He looked in front of him for some while before he spoke again. 'I've been a prisoner too long to count on anything,' he said, looking across the river. 'Do you remember all those early days in Lamsdorf, when the war ended every day, all those bloody rumours that made us think we would be out of it in a couple of months? Remember those rumours of repatriation a couple of years ago, when all prisoners taken in 1940 were going to be sent back home? No, I've been led up a gum tree too often to believe anything before it really happens.'

'It's not a rumour that the war is nearly over,' I said.

As Spot didn't answer, I took out of my pocket a hard-boiled egg that a guard had given me, and began to peel it. As I did so, the air-raid siren began to warble over Regensburg. Neither Spot nor I took much notice of it. Regensburg was a small town, and we couldn't really imagine it being of any interest to our planes.

But about ten minutes later we saw them high above us, hardly visible, with the sun on their wings. A few seconds later we saw the first marker drop over Regensburg, and we knew that the town was for it. We weren't worried for ourselves at all. Regensburg was quite a little way in front of us, just far enough to be safe, while we had a grandstand view of its bombing.

The first bombs dropped dead in the centre of Regensburg. The sounds of the explosions mingled into one mighty roar, and as a dense cloud of black smoke rose up from the town, everyone began to cheer wildly. Suddenly, there was a fresh droning sound above us, and looking up we saw another flight of planes was heading towards the town. They seemed to be moving very slowly. And then, quite suddenly, they were overhead. Something dropped from the first plane, and a second later a small trail of smoke hovered in the sky above us.

'Christ!' Spot whispered. 'It's a marker! They must be after the bridge!'

Even as he said it, I dropped the egg and began to roll down the slope towards the edge of the river. Spot was close behind me. The next moment we heard the bombs falling, whistling through the air and exploding along the river bank. And then it was over.

Slowly Spot and I climbed back up the bank. On the way up I began to search for the egg I dropped. Reaching the top of the bank we saw a great pall of smoke stretching along the river's edge, and through it the shattered ruins of the bridge.

'Well,' I said breathlessly. 'They got the bridge all right.'

'It's not the only thing they've got,' Spot said beside me.

And then I saw what he meant. As the great wisps of smoke began to clear, I could see the bodies of dead and wounded prisoners lying around the great bomb craters that pitted the bank.

We both sank down on the bank. With shaking fingers I took out a cigarette and lit it.

'The poor bastards!' Spot said softly beside me. 'They might have been free in a couple of weeks or so, if they had missed this lot. It's like I said, you can't trust anything to turn out right.'

As we sat there some of the prisoners who had been near the bridge began to come towards us, helping a few of the wounded along with them.

'I suppose we'd better go down and see if there's anything we can do,' Spot said.

Together we got up and began to walk along the river bank. Already some of the guards and prisoners had begun to examine the bodies, throwing a blanket or jacket over the faces of the dead. Quite near us lay someone with his head completely blown off, and farther along another prisoner was lying on his back beside a small shell-hole, killed by the concussion and without a mark on him.

'I don't think there's much sense in this,' I muttered to Spot. 'There's really nothing we can do, anyway.'

As we stood there, looking around us, I began to see that it was not only the prisoners who had suffered. Several guards were among the dead and dying that lay along the bank. As we turned to go back, a German guard passed us, chatting cheerfully to one of his comrades. Both his hands had been blown off at the wrists. I learned later that he had tried to get rid of the stick-grenades from his boots, fearing that the concussion from his boots might send them off. He had got as far as getting them out of his boots, when they had gone off in his hands.

Strangely enough, the guards completely changed from that moment. I saw quite a number of them going around the dying, putting cigarettes in their mouths and making them as comfortable as possible. They seemed as horrified as we were that so many should have died within sight of liberation. From that moment I never saw a guard raise his hand against a prisoner.

It was dusk when we set off again. The dead and the wounded had been transported to the hospital at Regensburg, and there were only the craters to show what had happened. We spent the whole of that night putting as much distance as possible between us and Regensburg. And as we trudged on, hour after hour, along winding paths that seemed to lead nowhere, we could hear above us the continuous drone of planes.

About nine o'clock the next morning we staggered into

the welcome haven of some barns just outside a village. No sooner had we got to sleep than we were awakened by the sound of guns and the heavy drone of bombers. We went outside just in time a see a plane diving down in flames. It landed and exploded perilously near the barns. With the German ack-ack so near, it was clear that the guards had not picked a very good place. So on we moved again.

From that moment every hour on the roads was a terrifying ordeal. We would march, very cautiously, in a single column on each side of the road, and then, just as we were congratulating ourselves on getting through the day without any trouble, a plane would come over and send us stampeding as the bombs dropped. We tried marching through the woods—but that was even worse. Any plane that went over, automatically machine-gunned them—just in case there were any German troops in them.

The French prisoners, always practical in matters of self-preservation, made themselves banners out of canvas marked with a red cross. These were carried on poles and displayed prominently for any plane that might come down with the intention of machine-gunning them. The British made no attempt to follow their example, but merely hoped for the best.

Ironically, it seemed that after surviving all that had gone before, we were now to be slowly wiped out by our own planes. At last it got so bad that we marched only by night and slept by day. But we were not even safe in the barns. Planes, seeing large groups in the farmyards—and the British would insist on moving about outside—would machine-gun the place or drop a bomb nearby. Finally, the British prisoners-of-war stirred themselves sufficiently to put whitewash prisoner-of-war signs on the roofs of the barns where they were staying. By that time, we were all in such a state of nerves that the slightest sound that bore any resemblance to the sound of a plane was enough to send us diving for cover.

The beginning of the end came quite unexpectedly. Starting off early one morning, we began to walk along a straight stretch of country road that lay between the Bavarian hills. It was a bright morning, quite hot for April, and we had no thought that liberation might be near. Since we had entered Bavaria, we had quite lost contact with the war, and we no longer had any idea where the Americans were.

Suddenly, ahead of us in the distance we saw a great field with large groups of British prisoners standing around in it. A few minutes later we were marching into the field to join them. As we straggled to a halt, Lober came forward to address us. He looked old and tired, and worse than I had ever seen him looking before.

'The marching is over,' Lober said. 'The American forces are now quite near, and it has been arranged for you to stay here until they come. We shall also stay with you and surrender ourselves to your comrades.' He looked at us for a moment, as if he were going to say something else, and then, turning on his heel, he walked towards the German guards already in the field, his own guards following him. He had only gone a little way when he turned suddenly. 'Good luck!' he said. And then he was walking away again.

As the day wore on, more and more prisoners arrived, Russians among them, until by the late afternoon, there were several hundreds of us in the field. By now, the guards were leaving us strictly to ourselves, and were sitting in subdued groups, waiting for their turn as prisoners-of-war. As dusk settled, however, several of the guards who had treated prisoners badly on the march, began to slip away. The end was indeed near.

As darkness fell and the prisoners began to settle down for the night, Spot and I went for a walk around the field. It was a beautiful, clear night, and despite the number of men in the field strangely quiet. We walked in silence for a long time.

'Well, Vinny boy,' Spot said finally. 'This really does look like the end, doesn't it?'

'We've waited a long time for it,' I said. 'A long, long time.'

'Excited?' Spot asked.

'It's funny,' I said. 'But I don't feel a thing. Except that I'm very tired.'

'That's how I feel,' Spot said. 'Let's go to bed.'

CHAPTER TWELVE

Liberation

THE next morning the Americans came.

As a nation with a flair for showmanship, the Americans should have arranged our liberation on a grander scale than they did. There should have been a marching army armed to the teeth, tanks roaring down the road in a cloud of dust, and a General, preferably Patton himself, coming into the field to officially liberate us with a few well-chosen words appropriate to the occasion.

Instead, there was only a solitary Sherman tank that came slowly down the road, its gun muzzle swinging enquiringly left and right as it approached us. When it reached the edge of the field it stopped, and an American officer clambered out of the turret and dropped lightly on to the road. He stood there for some moments, his hands on his hips, silently regarding the groups of equally silent prisoners watching him from the field.

It was not until the officer had waved a casual greeting that the silence was broken. With a loud cheer, some of the prisoners nearest the road bounded forward and surrounded the officer. They picked him up and threw him into the air. Not being very fit, they did not make a very good job of catching him as he came down again. Fortunately, the officer did not seem to mind. Picking himself up, he carefully brushed his tunic, and then grinned up at his crew, who had suddenly appeared above the turret and were now looking around them with rather a bored air. When the excitement had died down a little, the officer lifted his hand for silence, and everyone moved forward to hear what he had to say.

'Well, you're free, fellers,' the officer said. He seemed very young, very neat and smart in his uniform, his helmet pushed back rakishly. 'Our boys are in the village over there,' the officer went on, pointing behind him. 'But we want you to stay here until we get things sorted out a bit. I guess you won't mind that.'

Some of the German guards came forward slowly, their hands in the air. The officer frowned and waved them to go back. Quickly the guards retreated.

'You fellers can keep an eye on those Krauts,' the officer said, still frowning. 'And if you have any trouble with them, kill them. Meanwhile, just hang on here until you get further orders. When I get back to the village, I'll arrange for some food to be sent out to you.'

The officer clambered back into the tank, and a few moments later it was disappearing down the road.

'Well, now it's really happened,' Spot said softly beside me, 'do you feel any more excited about it?'

I shook my head. 'Now that it comes to the point, I find the thought of going back a little frightening,' I said. 'Everyone is going to seem like a stranger. It's not going to be easy to readjust ourselves after all these years we've spent working with Poles and Germans. I'm not even sure we think like Englishmen any more.'

'I don't know what you're worrying about,' Spot said. 'I'm just going to take things as they come.' He sighed. 'I reckon I've learnt a lot from being a prisoner-of-war. From now on I'll be quite happy to sit at home with the old carpet slippers on and a pipe stuck in my mouth.'

'That's all you want now,' I said. 'Once you're out of all this, you'll feel differently. You wait and see.'

We lapsed into silence and watched a group of prisoners striding purposefully across the field towards the guards, who now sat huddled together in the grass, apathetically waiting for something to happen to them. Surrounding the guards, the prisoners began to taunt them quietly. As I watched them, it suddenly struck me that the expressions on their faces were very much the same as those I had seen on the faces of some of the Germans who had taunted us as we walked through the French villages on our way to Germany.

'I don't know why they bother,' Spot said in disgust. 'Me —I'm just not interested in the guards any more. All I want to do now is to get back and forget all about it.'

Some of the Russians were now leaving the field and taking to the small footpath that led to the village. They moved slowly, walking along the path cautiously, keeping close to the trees that ran along one side of the path. Although they were now free men, they behaved as if they might run into serious trouble at any moment. In a way I could understand the reason for it. Liberated by the Americans, whom they mistrusted; ignored by most of the British, who still tended to be prejudiced by the years of German propaganda, they were a small minority, still living in enemy territory, with no one around them whom they felt they could trust. For them the war would not be over until they were back again with their own people.

Some hours later, while we were still waiting for the promised rations to arrive, the Russians returned, looking very pleased with themselves as they scuttled back into the field, carrying some large tins of meat and a couple of dead chickens. Squatting down, they immediately opened the tins with an old knife they had picked up from somewhere, and cutting the meat into thick slices, smilingly offered it to anyone who was near, irrespective of whether they were British or Russian.

The Russians who had made the raid on the village were all Mongols, rather frightening to look at, with their black, slit eyes peering out of faces that had been made wolfish-looking through months, possibly years, of starvation. But as I watched them squatting there, grinning broadly as they dished out their plunder to all and sundry, I could not help comparing them favourably with some of my fellow countrymen who had cheerfully robbed anyone they could on the march and who wouldn't give a crumb to anyone.

Shortly afterwards, a lorry came into the field, loaded up

with great sides of freshly killed pork. The pork was dropped off the lorry for us to cut up and distribute among ourselves the best way we could, while the two American soldiers who had come with the lorry went off to collect the guards. The guards got up slowly from the grass as they saw the two American soldiers approaching them. One of the Americans jerked a laconic thumb, and the guards began to walk quickly towards the lorry in a tight, compact bunch, each one of them probably calculating that while he was close to the others there was less chance of being singled out for any unpleasant attentions from the two American soldiers. From past experience I knew just how they felt. Only Schmidt, the Unteroffizier, walked alone. Bringing up the rear, he strolled without haste across the field, looking thoughtfully at the grass. As he walked past me, I stepped forward and fell into step beside him. One of the Americans looked as if he was going to say something, but didn't.

'Ah, Vincent,' Schmidt said, looking up as I joined him. 'You said the day might come when I would be behind the wire and you outside it. How right you were.'

'Ah well,' I said. 'You won't be a prisoner as long as I was. It won't be long before you're back in Vienna in charge of that wonderful *Gasthaus* of yours.'

Schmidt smiled wryly and said nothing.

When we reached the lorry I held out my hand and Schmidt took it. '*Glück Auf*,' I said. '*Und Leben Sie wohl.*'

Schmidt clambered into the lorry with the others. The driver revved his engine, and the two American soldiers banged up the tailboard and then clambered in with the guards. A moment later the lorry was bumping across the field towards the road. Schmidt waved once or twice, and then sank out of sight behind the tailboard.

Some years later, when I was in Vienna, I saw the name of Schmidt over a *Gasthaus*, and as I stood there looking up at the familiar name above the door, the memories came flooding back. With one foot on the front step of the *Gasthaus*, I thought of Kristina and of some of the friends I had left behind me in Poland, and I wondered what they were doing now. But I did not go in to find out how Herr Schmidt was prospering. There is always a sadness in looking back on past things, even bad things that are over and almost forgotten, and I knew that a long talk on the old days with Schmidt would only be depressing. Taking my foot off the step, I walked away.

The consignment of pork which the Americans had sent us provided a disastrous ending to the day by bringing the lot of us down with acute diarrhœa. Pork was out of season in the first place, but as we had only half cooked it over twig fires and then gobbled down great chunks, we really only had ourselves to blame.

Night fell, and like everyone else I spent most of it lying groaning on the dew-sodden grass, getting up at frequent intervals to make a frantic dash for the nearest bushes.

The sun came up soon after dawn. With my bowels still in command of the situation, I sat beside Spot, idly watching the groups of men already wandering aimlessly around the field. Through the distant trees beyond the road I caught a glimpse of the village, a church tower and some red, one-storied houses, their grey tiles shimmering in the early morning sun. Outside the village were a few scattered farms, and something that looked like an air-field. It all seemed very peaceful.

But although the village looked quiet enough, the Americans did not come to tell us that we could enter it. The day wore on and nothing happened. A single plane droned across the clear sky above us, circled the field, and then went back the same way it had come. We walked and we talked, and we waited until the sun went down—and there was still no sign of the Americans or any further rations.

Growing tired of pacing up and down the field, I went over to a group of Russians, hoping that I might be able to strike up some form of conversation with them. Most of them talked pidgin-German, and one of them even knew

English, which he spoke haltingly through lack of practice, but very correctly. The Russians told me of the atrocities that had been committed in their camps, and also of some of the things that the Germans had done to the Russian civilians when they had first advanced into Russia. As they talked, their faces wore that look of dedicated hatred which I had seen on the faces of some of the Poles whenever they had spoken of the Germans.

When dusk came, the Russians gathered together to discuss something, talking very seriously among themselves and at some length. Soon afterwards, they began to leave the field and head towards the village, this time taking the pathetic scraps of their belongings with them. Before the last of them had left, the British had also begun to move out, fed up at last with sitting around waiting for something to happen.

We found the village swarming with American troops, but otherwise quite peaceful. The officers seemed slightly surprised to see us, and rather at a loss to know what to do with us now that we had arrived. Their final decision was a little unsatisfactory. Dig in where we could and scrounge food from where we could. We were, however, not to force ourselves on the German civilians if they did not want us, nor were we to steal their food. There were quite a lot of farms in the village, and if necessary we could sleep in the barns. The war suddenly seemed a little cock-eyed.

As it happened, we had no trouble in finding accommodation. The arrival of the Russians had thrown the womenfolk into a blind panic, and as there was hardly a single German male in the village beyond a few ancients and cripples, they were only too pleased to take an Englishman into the house as a protection against the admittedly rather fearsome-looking Russians who stalked the village. Within an hour or so, most of us were settled comfortably in the houses and farms in and around the village. Spot had managed to find himself a room in a farm, and I had parked myself on a middle-aged German woman who had practically dragged me into the house when I had asked her for a room. Her name was Frau Schröber.

Frau Schröber was a rather unusual woman to find tucked away in a small village. She spoke almost perfect English, was cultured, and had travelled widely. Her husband —Oberleutnant Schröber—had been reported missing on the Russian Front in 1943, and had never been heard of again. Frau Schröber still grieved for him very much. According to Frau Schröber he had been a very wonderful man. Now, as she told me, he was gone, and all she had to remember him by were her memories and a single picture of him. The black-draped picture of Oberleutnant Schröber hung in the parlour, a granite-faced man wearing the Iron Cross. Oberleutnant Schröber looked a bastard, but I did not tell his wife that.

I was rather surprised to hear that Frau Schröber had been very much against the Nazi régime, and had listened to the English news regularly, a crime for which she could have been punished by death. I knew that she was not lying when she told me this, for she spoke of things which I had heard on our wireless in the camp but which had not been published in the German newspapers.

After we had talked late into the night, I ate the bowl of soup that Frau Schröber had prepared for me, and then saying good night, I went up to my room to sleep in my first real bed in five years. I should have slept like a log in the huge bed that awaited me, but the all-enveloping German feather mattress and eiderdown practically suffocated me, and in the end I got up and slept on the floor.

When I got up the next morning and went to the window, I found myself looking on to the air-field I had seen from the field on the previous day. It was quite deserted and had the appearance of having been abandoned in a hurry, the black mouths of the hangars gaping open and empty, the field desolate except for the burnt-out remains of a solitary German plane lying on the grass near the runway. Lying farther back were the Luftwaffe barracks, black-creosoted huts with curtains at the windows.

Later that morning the Americans began working on the field, and in no time at all they had cleared away the wrecked plane, set up ack-ack guns on the edge of the field, and had established an American Red Cross headquarters on the far side of the field. As soon as it became known that the Americans had set up a Red Cross H.Q., a great horde of prisoners advanced upon it to see what they could scrounge. The American women running it were very sweet but rather vague. We came away clutching some American magazines and a few packets of chewing-gum—not exactly our idea of a good haul.

The next afternoon I was settling down in the bedroom for a quiet nap, when the faint hum of approaching planes made me get up and go to the window. Looking out I saw two black specks moving through the sky, the sound of their approach little more than a vibration in the air, as they headed slowly towards the air-field. As the droning of their engines grew louder, Frau Schröber rushed up the stairs and joined me by the window.

'The boys are coming home,' Frau Schröber cried. 'Look, the boys are coming home.'

The two planes began to circle the field, gradually coming lower and lower. The ack-ack guns started up and shells began to burst above the planes, little black puffs of smoke that were quickly whisked away in the high wind. The two planes continued to circle the field, still coming lower all the time. The ack-ack guns stopped suddenly. It was clear that the planes were going to land. The first plane came zooming over the house and then landed on the runway. A perfect landing. The sound of the engine died away as it was cut off and a German Luftwaffe pilot stepped out of the plane and then walked slowly across the field to the waiting Americans. Beside me, Frau Schröber wept softly.

'I used to watch them leave this field every day,' Frau Schröber said, wiping the tears from her eyes. 'Many of them were such young boys, and so often they went up and did not return. It was very sad. Now the last of them are coming home for good, and they will never fly away from here again.'

'Thank God for that,' I said, watching the other plane land.

Frau Schröber sighed and said nothing. She left me standing at the window and went downstairs. A few moments later I followed her down, thinking that this was perhaps a good time to get her views on one or two things. I found her in the kitchen, placidly sorting out some cotton and thread in her work-basket.

'Frau Schröber,' I said, sitting down at the table opposite her. 'You say you hated the Nazi régime, so perhaps I can talk without giving offence. You know, I have never been able to understand how the Germans were capable of doing some of the things they did. The Russians, for instance——'

'The Russians are animals,' Frau Schröber interrupted me fiercely. 'Look how they walk the streets of this village like wild beasts.' She shuddered. 'Like wild beasts!' she whispered. Frau Schröber's fear of the Russians was very genuine.

'Well, I still don't understand any of it,' I said. 'You're cultured people and supposed to be civilized. I've met kind people among you—lots of kind people. And I can't reconcile it with all the atrocities I've heard of and the concentration camps.'

'Ordinary German people cannot be held responsible for what happened in those places,' Frau Schröber said firmly.

I couldn't really believe it for a moment. I looked at Frau Schröber to see if she was being serious. I saw that she was quite serious.

'Of course, people who have been in the punishment camps will exaggerate it, anyway,' Frau Schröber continued. 'It must have been very unpleasant for them. But there are cruel people everywhere, who will do things to other people they have at their mercy.' Frau Schröber shook her head.

'But you can't judge the German people by them. Not the real German people.' She smiled. 'Now, if you will give me your shirt, I will mend it so that you will look nice when you return to your people.'

I could see there was no point in pursuing the subject, so I dropped it. I took off my shirt and gave it to Frau Schröber, and she began to get busy with her needle and cotton. I could see that it gave her genuine pleasure to think she was helping to smarten me up for going home. The Germans never failed to amaze me.

Later that afternoon two more planes came in to surrender. The pilots were young, little more than boys, but as they stepped out of their planes and walked across the runway towards captivity, I noticed that they walked with the same slightly self-conscious swagger that I had seen in older Luftwaffe pilots when they walked the streets.

After those first two days of freedom, the other days that follow go by much more slowly; hot, boring days with nothing to do but trail up and down the village or lay in the garden dozing in the sun while we wait for the planes that are going to take us home. We have now been told that the planes will definitely be taking us from here, but no one is quite sure when that will be. So all we can do is to sit around and wait. It is a funny thing, but being free again already doesn't seem so wonderful as it should be. I am beginning to realize that freedom in itself is useless unless you can employ it somehow, not necessarily in being useful, but at least in doing something. Spot is quite wrong in thinking that a pair of carpet slippers and a pipe are going to be enough.

The Russians seem to have gone to earth completely, but occasionally some of them can be seen in the village, slouched against the walls or searching the gutters for butts that the American troops have thrown away. If the Americans do not seem to know what to do with us, they have even less idea of what to do with the Russians. No one feeds them, of course, so they live by stealing, clambering into the back gardens at night to wring the neck of a chicken, and then disappearing over the fence like wraiths before the chicken's final death squawk has brought someone to the window. It is very regrettable that a number of British prisoners now take their role as protectors of German property very seriously, and sad to see them behaving like indignant landlords as they chase the Russians out of the vegetable plots and chicken-runs, while the Frau of the house looks on with tight-lipped approval. Sad, because they have forgotten so quickly, and sad because the Russians will not very quickly forget those Britons who drove them away.

Maybe the years of imprisonment have soured us, but we do not seem to like anyone much these days, not even the Americans who liberated us. They more or less ignore us in the street, and if you approach them for a cigarette they will give you one all right, perhaps even give you a full packet, but without much grace and very much in the same abstract way as you would drop a copper into the hat of a beggar. I suppose they look upon us rather in the same way as some of us look upon the Russians.

We have just heard that it is now safe for us to go into Landshut if we wish. Although Landshut is more than ten miles away, I have decided that I must go there quickly. We are getting short of food in the house, Frau Schröber and I, and I want to get into Landshut before the rest of the prisoners strip the town clean of anything that might be had from there. As I had no intention of going there on foot, I stole a bicycle and cycled there, taking with me a huge sack that I had found in Frau Schröber's kitchen.

Not wishing to be bothered with the bike in town, I left it at a house on the outskirts, with strict instructions for it to be looked after carefully until I came back to collect it. As I went out on the road again, I saw an Englishman sitting on a wall opposite. He must have got off the mark very quickly to have got there before me. We both waved to each other, and then I crossed over the bridge that led into Landshut.

Much of Landshut is a mass of rubble and ruins, the road blocked with great lumps of fallen masonry. Although many of the houses are now only gutted shells, there are others with only the front wall missing, leaving the bedrooms intact, almost tidy, except for the fallen plaster on the floors and the splintered laths that droop down from the damaged roofs. The Americans are already at work clearing the roads, and doing it very efficiently by the looks of it, as they work in gangs, breaking up the stones and shovelling the rubble into waiting lorries. The M.P.'s and the German police work side by side, controlling the rubble-loaded lorries as they thread their way among the ruins. Quite a number of German civilians are out and about, not looking particularly shattered by what has happened to them. In fact, to see them standing on the kerbs watching the Americans at work, you would think they were watching them building the town instead of watching someone who has knocked it down.

Picking my way through the rubble, I continued my search for food. A young American soldier came towards me, a gun-belt dangling almost to his knees as he slouched along from hip to hip, like Gary Cooper. He seemed friendly-looking, so I stopped him.

'Where can I find some food in this town?' I said.

He waved a hand expansively around the ruins. 'Help yourself to anything you can find,' he said. 'The town's all yours.'

It was very nice of him to say so, but the town was far from being mine. All the shops were shut and there were M.P.'s everywhere to prevent looting. I was beginning to think that the sack I had brought with me was not only too large but a complete waste of time.

I had more or less given up looking for food, when I suddenly stumbled across an army cookhouse that had been erected on an open patch of ground among the ruins. Seeing the large tent marked 'Mess Hall', I galloped over the rubble and breathlessly came to a halt in front of the two copper boilers that were steaming away in front of the tent. As I hovered around the boilers, my nostrils twitching, two cooks came out from the tent and eyed me in that suspicious way that all army cooks look at anyone intruding on cookhouse territory out of eating hours.

'Well?' one of them said uncompromisingly.

'I'm looking for food,' I said.

They both studied me thoughtfully. Then one of them went into the tent and emerged with two P.K. packs which he handed to me without saying a word. Thanking him, I dropped the two packs into my sack. They looked rather lost in the bottom of it.

After the two cooks had retired into the mess hall, I prowled around the cookhouse, hoping I might find something else to take back to Frau Schröber. I was thinking ambitiously in terms of a small carcase of meat, but all that I found were several hundreds of little boxes of boiled sweets that had been dumped carelessly on the ground at the back of the mess hall. Half filling the sack with them, I humped it on my back and quickly retreated.

The sack was heavy, and I was grateful to reach the house where my bike was waiting for me. The woman with whom I had left it seemed surprised to see me when she opened the door.

'My bicycle, please,' I said.

'But it has gone,' the woman said.

'What do you mean, it's gone?' I said irritably.

'Your comrade called here for it a few minutes after you left,' the woman said. 'He told me that you said it would be in order for him to take it.'

I suddenly remembered the Englishman to whom I had waved on entering Landshut.

Seeing the expression on my face the woman said anxiously: 'Did I do wrong?'

'It doesn't matter,' I said wearily. I looked down the long

stretch of road awaiting me. It was going to be a long walk.

I crawled into the house some hours later, feeling that the trip had hardly been worth it. Finding Frau Schröber in the kitchen, I emptied the boxes of sweets on to the table. 'You'd better give these out among the village children,' I said. 'Keep some for us, of course.'

The two P.K. packs came out of the sack last, and after Frau Schröber had recovered from her joyful hysterics over the coffee that was in them, she remembered that Spot had called while I had been away in Landshut.

'Your comrade came around with some friends to tell you that the Americans are giving a film show to the troops this evening,' she said. 'They will call for you again at seven.'

I had seen only one film show since I had been captured, a dreary programme that the Germans had hawked around most of the working parties. It had consisted of a film of the 1936 Olympics, carefully cut so as to show how the Germans and the Japanese had won all the events, and a turgid comedy that looked as if it had been made at the same time as the Olympic Games film. There had been an arch heroine and two German comics, one bald-headed and gross, the other dapper, with a clearly pencilled moustache. They had all spent most of the film running in and out of the bedroom and bathroom. The prospect of seeing an up-to-date American film was therefore an agreeable one.

That night, when Spot and some of the other prisoners came to collect me, I had washed and shaved with particular care, and was wearing a freshly pressed shirt that Frau Schröber had ironed for me. As I left the house, Frau Schröber produced a packet of German cigarettes and pressed them into my hand. To help make a real evening of it, Frau Schröber said. In many ways I was beginning to like Frau Schröber.

We arrived at the hall where the film show was to be held to find some sort of argument going on outside between an American officer and a number of Britishers who had arrived there before us. The American troops also there, waiting for the doors to be opened, were listening interestedly to the argument.

'I'm sorry,' the officer was saying, 'but all the seats are reserved for our fellers. Most of them haven't seen a film for some time.'

'The poor dears,' someone said sarcastically, 'we haven't seen one for five years.'

'I'm sorry,' the officer said tightly, 'but you can't go in.'

For a moment I thought there was going to be a fight. Some of the Britishers began making some very rude remarks about the Americans, and immediately most of the American soldiers started to cluster around the officer. Fortunately, nothing came of it. The British continued to mutter and scowl angrily among themselves, with the Americans watching them warily, until finally, the tension was broken by the doors of the hall clanging open. Slowly the Americans began to file into the hall. We watched them go until there was only the officer standing outside.

'Sorry,' he said. And then he went into the hall and the door closed behind him.

The incident, small in itself, has served only to widen the gulf that is already between us. Now no one can find a good word to say for the Americans. We speak among ourselves of how spoilt they are, how soft they are, forgetting that they have fought their way across Germany, leaving hundreds of their dead behind them, and therefore have some right to enjoy themselves. Of course, we too have come a long way in more ways than one, to reach this backwater. But that does not entitle us to more consideration than anyone else because of it. A lot of ex-prisoners seem to feel that someone owes them something. What, they are not quite sure, but something. They have yet to learn that no one owes them anything. Now that it is all over, we were lucky to have been prisoners, if only by the very fact of our survival.

The food problem has been solved by the magical arrival of Red Cross parcels, which shows at least that we have not been abandoned and forgotten like the Russians, who are still here, living as best they can until someone gets down to the problem of dealing with them.

Finally the planes came, nine Lancaster bombers that roared out of the sky, and then landed, one by one, their great wings glistening in the sun as they slowly taxied around to prepare to take off again. No one has been warned of their coming, not even the Americans, for at the very moment that the planes are landing, a jeep is running up and down the village, an officer standing up in the jeep, shouting for us to make for the air-field as quickly as possible. The first men there will be the first to go. There are only nine planes, and as no one knows when the next ones will arrive there is a wild exodus from houses and farms until the whole street is filled with men racing madly towards the air-field.

There is hardly time to say good-bye to Frau Schröber; a few gabbled words of thanks, Frau Schröber's stout arm flung around my shoulder for a moment, and then down the path to join the mass evacuation from the village.

'Good-bye, Frau Schröber,' I cried as I ran down the path. 'Good-bye.' As I stopped at the gate for a moment and looked back, I saw that Frau Schröber was crying.

With Frau Schröber's house so near the air-field, I had no difficulty in getting a place on one of the waiting planes. As I clambered into it, I was pleased to see Spot leading the way towards one of the other planes. A few minutes later the plane was climbing up into the sky and heading westwards. First stop Brussels.

We arrived in Brussels late in the afternoon. Lorries took us to some old Belgian barracks now occupied by the British, and there we were handed over to some very sympathetic Sergeant-Majors. There were forms to fill in and questions to answer, but everyone was very kind and helpful. After that, free tea and cigarettes in the Naafi and five pounds for each man to spend in town. But not on the prostitutes, boys. Remember your wives and sweethearts are waiting for you.

THE LONG ROAD HOME

After spending an evening going around the local bars, I returned to the barracks to await the dawn and the plane that was going to take me to England. The only thing to mar a perfect day was the news that a plane carrying prisoners home had crashed on landing in England. All killed. Such rotten luck.

The next morning I was on the plane, heading for England.

The sun is on the wings and below is the English Channel. Perhaps at this moment I should be thinking of home and all the things I am going to do when I get back. But I don't want to think about anything, only relax. I don't suppose there will ever be a moment like this again for me, and I want to make the most of it. Already the cliffs of England are beginning to emerge from the June haze.

THE END